ADVANCE PRAISE

"It is often said of someone that they come from a 'colorful' family, a description which will seem like a radical overstatement once one has read Erin Chandler's remarkable *BLUEGRASS SONS*, a memoir populated by gamblers, smugglers, drug dealers, CIA agents, murderers, prostitutes and a cast of characters so far removed from the 'normal' as to warrant an entirely new definition of that term.

Here is an embodiment of Philip Roth's well-known statement that we no longer have much need for fiction, since reality provides us with more than enough strangeness and incredulity to satisfy those needs. No one could have invented a story stranger than Erin Chandler's family's, nor filled it with more remarkable characters, and now, gratefully, no one has to."

—Michael Blumenthal, *From Exile to Washington: A Memoir of Leadership in the Twentieth Century, Don't Die: Poems 2013-2021, Against Romance*

"Insider and survivor, Erin Chandler vigorously questions the accepted news coverage of a notorious conspiracy of drugs, murder, and money, all entangled with the twisted charm of the Kentucky Bluegrass. She recalls her innocent childhood encounters with 'normal people', whom she later learned were ruthless drug lords and killers. The shock of revelation is palpable in her memories and in her prose. Never wavering in her loyalty to her family, Ms. Chandler pursues the other story, the untold story, the true story that so violently rewrote her personal fairy tale."

—Kevin Lane Dearinger, *Bad Sex in Kentucky, On Stage with Bette Davis, The Bard in the Bluegrass*

ALSO BY ERIN CHANDLER:

June Bug Versus Hurricane

Cinderella Sweeping Up: A Collection of Essays

Bluegrass Sons

RABBIT HOUSE PRESS
Versailles, KY 40383

Published in the United States by Rabbit House Press,
September 2024, Revised edition June 2025. Printed in the
United States of America.

For inquiries about author appearances and/or volume orders contact:
Emily Wilhoit or Kristin Minter at rabbithousepress@gmail.com

ISBN: 979-8-9907833-3-1

Edited by: Leigh Bryant Stevenson
Final copy edit: Brooke Lee
Special thanks to University Press of Kentucky Peer Readers
Interior and cover design: Brooke Lee
Graphic asset on dust jacket by Vecteezy.com

Bluegrass Sons

A True Crime Memoir

Erin Chandler

RABBIT
HOUSE
PRESS
rabbithousepress.com

For Uncle Brad

1944—2024

PROLOGUE

"The things I'm going to tell you, you'll never look at me the same way again," my uncle stared at the ground, "there's nothing fun about it, it's a fucking horror story." We ambled around the baseball diamond in downtown Southern Pines, North Carolina as he walked me through it, the smugglers, the agents, the murderers and justifications, the slow burn of duty. A treasure chest of regret and resolve began to unravel as I tugged at the ball of string in which my uncle's lies were tangled. "Your lies are your life," he said sternly. "My lies are my life."

Piecing together my mother's younger brother, Bradley Fred Bryant's secret life and his choice to exist in a world of darkness is a puzzle. It is a puzzle our family keeps on the shelf behind the Monopoly and Scrabble, hidden in back with the Ouija Board. We know it's there, but opening could unleash a torrential flood of demons. "To kill a monster sometimes you have to get in bed with other monsters," said DEA agent Steve Murphy in the Netflix drama *Narcos*. "If that surprises you, pick up a history book. It's what we do."

As Uncle Brad explained the decade in question, 1970-1980, he was careful to protect my father, his brother-in-law. My parents divorced when I was eight years old after fifteen years of marriage, but an unshakable bond between Brad Bryant and Dan Chandler had already been formed. Full lives and a mountain of history was acquired before their unconventional lifestyles intersected out west. When Uncle Brad shed a long-covered light on our family dynamic, it was more complicated than I ever imagined. So complicated, many people heavily involved refused to talk. My dad's longtime girlfriend, witness to all, sent a message that it was "a hard no" when asked if she would discuss Uncle Brad, Daddy, and the infamous Chagra brothers.

"You want to think you're good people," Uncle Brad said. "Think you are." Everyone has their own version of truth regarding the glamorous drama that played out in the 1970s and early 80s. As the characters moved seamlessly between Lexington, Miami and Las Vegas, Philadelphia, El Paso and Savannah, Colombia, Guatemala, and Nicaragua, fortunes were made and careers were crushed, people went to prison and others died mysterious deaths. I reached out to the key players, lawyers, CIA and FBI experts, family, friends, governors and other eyewitnesses, recording their memories. Most enlightening was hearing my uncle recount his undercover life. I remember the people and places of which he spoke. That decade spanned my pre-teen and teenage years when my brother and I shadowed our father's every move while living with him during summers and holidays in and around Caesar's Palace in Las Vegas. I recalled easily the personalities if not the darkest deeds.

In 2020, thirty years after Uncle Brad's release from federal prison, he was in a different kind of isolation. With the coronavirus pandemic raging outside our doors, we examined his life during a series of conversations. The man who once carried commando daggers, secret identities and Russian-English dictionaries quietly faced a forest of pine trees outside his wall of windows. Sitting in front of the computer, Uncle Brad's spine is rigid and in impeccable alignment. Tiny veins are visible atop his perfectly shaved head. He laughs easily but is still wound tight as a drum, seriousness is ever-present, his stern wrath a heartbeat away.

PART I

DARK ALLIANCE

Dan Chandler 'on both ends of the bench' with criminal defense attorney and good friend, Lee Chagra.

CHAPTER
ONE

"Teach a man a craft and he's liable to practice it..."
—Gary Webb

Eli Cohen was a spy. In fact, he was known as Israel's greatest spy. In the 1960s there was a battle between Israel and its Arab neighbors in Syria over the water source of the Jordan River. The river originated in Arab territory but provided Israel with much needed irrigation to thrive in the dry atmosphere. Eli was fearless and selfless in pursuit of a cause, providing impossible to get intelligence to the Israeli government for years. When his true identity was uncovered by Syrian counterintelligence, he was hung in the public square.

My mother, Lynne Bryant Chandler, recalls her first initial feeling that something was terribly wrong with the path her brother was on. "It was at the Lexington, Kentucky airport in the private plane section," she remembered. "Your dad was with Brad. I don't know how I knew Jimmy Chagra was on the plane, but I knew Bradley was involved with Jimmy. First of all, Brad looked so smoothy with his leather jacket. It didn't look like him. It didn't make me think about the way he really was. Your Daddy came off the plane first and I remember saying, 'if you love Brad, you will get him away from those people.' Dan just hugged me and said, Bradsy's fine."

"She didn't know we were trying to get closer to him," Uncle Brad laughed when I recounted his sister's memory.

"Did Daddy know you were working for the government?" I asked.

"No. Hell no," Uncle Brad said. "He had no idea. Nope."

Brad was playing a part, undercover as that slick, cool cat in the caramel-colored leather jacket. A painstaking process brought my uncle to that moment on the Lexington tarmac. It was only a year before that Daddy had greeted him at the Las Vegas McCarran Airport. Waving from a Caesar's limo, my father was unaware of the task Brad was given by the CIA. Dan Chandler ushered him into the most exclusive areas of his new playground, no holds barred.

Brad Bryant was not your typical Vegas patron. He was not a gambler or a drinker, not particularly interested in the shows or the women. Unlike most desert dwellers who find themselves in a frigid casino amidst a world of green felt and black ties, Brad wasn't interested in the plethora of hedonistic pleasures before him. He was on a strict mission to infiltrate Jimmy Chagra's drug operation. It was a laborious, methodical process that demanded the utmost patience. He began by informing my father he was open for business, a security business. Next step was to wait for an introduction to Caesar's highest rollers, Lee and Jimmy Chagra. Gaining their confidence would be an undeniably dangerous job.

Lee Chagra. Jimmy Chagra. The Family Chagra. What comes to my mind when I think of the Chagras? My entire childhood. What comes to mind is walking through the casino, the cacophony of slot machines ringing in my ears, dripping from the pool, cold air chilling my legs. I remember wandering into the coffee shop like it was my own kitchen, passing hostesses who knew me by name, plopping into an orange booth with my father and his friend, the handsome, criminal defense attorney from El Paso, Lee Chagra. The Lebanese charmer had wide, dark eyes and gold necklaces, a white suit and white cowboy hat. He always winked at the waitress and ordered a club sandwich. There was a telephone on the table my father was unquestionably on, the old-fashioned kind, beige and square with a circular dial. Throughout the entire 70s, 80s and well into the 90s you could hear Daddy's name booming throughout the casino every few minutes, "Paging Mr. Chandler, Mr. Dan Chandler please. Paging Mr. Chandler, Mr. Dan Chandler."

Author Erin Chandler (center) with her father, Dan Chandler and Trish Turner, Andy William's backup singer/dancer, Caesar's Palace circa 1977

CHAPTER
TWO

Master of Ceremonies

"Dan Chandler was the host of hosts," Oscar Goodman, three-time Las Vegas mayor and infamous criminal defense attorney, said as he remembered my father. "He was beloved. Everybody in Las Vegas was his brother or his sister. Everybody wanted to be part of Dan Chandler. He was a sterling citizen. He was the best at what he did, and he enjoyed every single second."

It's impossible to over emphasize the ferocious wit and fearless magnetism of Joseph Daniel Chandler, how he fit so effortlessly into such diverse and exclusive circles. Daddy was born and raised in the governor's mansion with a father they called Happy. My grandfather, Albert Benjamin 'Happy' Chandler was a wildly popular twice–elected Kentucky governor and United States senator. Perhaps most significantly he integrated the schools in Kentucky and served as the second ever Baseball Commissioner who broke the color lines of organized baseball when he went against twelve of the thirteen club owners and supported Jackie Robinson's entry into the Major Leagues. Happy Chandler, or Pappy as we call him, is prominently featured in the Baseball Hall of Fame. Daddy idolized his father and used to joke, "I was born at the top and clawed my way to the middle!" That was a typical humble assessment. In truth, Joseph Daniel Chandler had charisma, innate charm, empathy and *joie de vivre* that surpassed my grandfather.

"I had a head start with Daddy," Dan Chandler said in a 2004 interview, "I had a head start being Daddy's son and I carried that out to Las Vegas." Following my parents' separation in 1969, my father made smooth transitions from the political and society set in Kentucky to running the tennis establishment at the Jockey Club in Miami, to casino host at Caesar's Palace in Las Vegas. Cliff Perlman, a friend and significant investor in the Jockey Club was president of Caesar's Palace at the time and offered Daddy employment out west as a casino host. With perfect grades in English and history while failing math and science, a future in the strict world of business was a disastrous foregone conclusion for the rambunctious governor's son. Daddy managed a brokerage company in Lexington and tried his hand at politics, running for Congress. He got involved with a chicken franchise and a few other financial ventures with his old 'frenemy,' future Kentucky governor, John Y. Brown Jr., but nothing held his attention.

In 1970, when the occupation came along to entertain people, give away hotel suites, free dinners, and show tickets at Caesar's Palace in Las Vegas, Nevada, Dan Chandler found his sweet spot. According to the men who gave my father this shining opportunity, his central responsibility was to find customers like Lee and Jimmy Chagra with disposable incomes and charm them into spending their cash at Caesar's. He advanced at record pace, going from having a small desk at the entrance between the check-in counter and a sea of Blackjack tables to becoming Vice President of the groundbreaking resort.

"Your dad was brilliant," Uncle Brad smiled. "He was absolutely brilliant. He could walk across the room and accomplish more in twenty steps than you would make in the next six months. He was brilliant. Complete character."

On a typical evening in Las Vegas as I went from a child to a teenager, it was champagne and caviar on ice delivered by women in skimpy Roman costumes with giant cone-shaped breasts and sky-high wigs braided at the crown to match their own brunette, crimson, or platinum tresses. Las Vegas in the 70s and 80s had another thing to offer which I latched on to for dear life. My father had a passion that surpassed all else and that was music and entertainment. He was granted all-access visits backstage after historic performances by Sammy Davis Jr., Tom Jones, Ann Margaret, and Frank Sinatra, becoming fast friends with them all. He formed a deep and lasting relationship with Andy Williams and The Lennon Sisters who also had residencies at Caesar's and came again and again for weeks at a time. Daddy fostered and encouraged my predilection for the arts and brought me to rehearsals during the daytime, waltzing me right backstage to watch the preparations, and ushering me to the front of the stage in the evenings to watch with the audience. Circus Maximus Showroom and its show people served as both babysitter and inspiration for my own life on stage and screen decades later.

I was awestruck when Andy Williams belted out "MacArthur Park" and Sammy Davis Jr. sang "Mr. Bojangles" while dancing on air, high lonesome screaming from his soul. Sometimes we saw two performances a night from big red booths in the middle of the showroom or right up front, my elbow resting on the vibrating stage itself. Depending on the week it might have been Paul Anka, Glen Campbell or Steve Lawrence and Eydie Gormé. If we weren't in the showroom at Caesar's, we were up the strip at the Tropicana, Sands or Desert Inn. Dan Chandler, this host of hosts, joyfully pointed out to his daughter the backup dancers wiggling in unison, so excited was he with their confidence and wild playfulness, "You think they're having fun?" he'd ask me with happy tears in his eyes. Wayne Newton brought us together in another way as he sang, "Daddy, Don't You Walk So Fast." My father held my hand, his ice blue eyes overflowing with a new mix of emotions. After each performance we sauntered backstage like we owned the place to meet the stars, then dine with them at the Ah So or Bacchanal. It was all showbiz all the time.

Back in the casino, I watched my father from a distance patting the backs and laughing with the Chagra brothers and their splashy entourage who were roped off at the Baccarat tables. The Chagras traveled with an enormous amount of cash and stacked it against the silky walls of the Frank Sinatra Suite in Caesar's. It was well known that the flamboyant brothers had a penchant for cocktail waitresses and occasionally paid off entire mortgages as a tip. When I think of the family, what comes to mind is flying in Caesar's private jet to the Kentucky Derby. I think of Lee Chagra's loving wife, son and daughters with their giant, white smiles, exuding warmth, protection, generosity and flash, flashy planes, flashy hotel suites, and flashy jewelry. Daddy and Lee were close friends from the moment they met. What started as a friendship between gambler and casino host became a whirlwind party defining the time, two men sucking the marrow out of the seventies, flying high on trunks of cash, buckets of Scotch Whiskey, cocaine, and marijuana. It was all very exciting but criminal and ultimately detrimental to all involved.

"What were the specifics of the mission the CIA gave you in the case of Lee and Jimmy Chagra?" I questioned Uncle Brad.

"Basically, initially, was to try to introduce ourselves, get ourselves in with these so-called 'connections' which turned out to be the Chagras," he said. "We had to get to the Chagras before we could do anything else. That in itself was a very complicated, step by step process there. I had to be in touch with your father and make time… take that step."

This was a double-edged sword. I couldn't objectively process this undercover operation. Introduce ourselves, try to get to know, get in with, all smacked of cold calculation and straight up lying to my father. Dan Chandler was a sitting duck, a resource in a CIA sting. In the eyes of the government men guiding this military man towards his mission, Daddy was simply low hanging fruit to get to Lee and Jimmy Chagra.

Uncle Brad was well on the road toward this double life of secrecy. While I know he loved my father and would never want to endanger him, another force drove his actions. A series of events created this tough kid and ultimate strong man. I came to believe Brad's father, my grandfather, Gene Bryant, who fought in Germany and France in World War II, primed my uncle for a life of service to our country in whatever form that might take. High school at the Sewanee Military Academy in Tennessee instilled a set of similar beliefs, and the United States Marines cemented his mentality of following orders and fulfilling duty. In no uncertain terms, Brad Bryant was trained to play the long game.

Bluegrass Sons

Wilma Seavey Bradley on the vaudeville
stage with her sister Mildred, early 1900's

Angelee Bradley Bryant

Angelee and Gene Bryant
on their wedding day

Bradley, Lynne and Earl Bryant

CHAPTER
THREE

This Story of Us

Regarding southern gentility, you needn't look further than my maternal grandmother, Angelee Bradley Bryant, who we called Dear. Dear looked like a movie star, a natural beauty with a cherub face, blonde curls, and Bette Davis Eyes. She was so tiny they joked she could sit on a dime and see the edges all the way around. Angelee Bradley grew up in an antebellum mansion in Versailles, Kentucky. Dear's mother, my great grandmother, Wilma Seavey Bradley, who we called Muwee, was a gorgeous, vaudevillian actress. She was plucked from the stage at fourteen by Ben Bradley, who had started the first Lyric theatre in Birmingham, Alabama. He convinced her to run away with him by saying if she didn't, he was going to China. Ben married Wilma and brought her to Kentucky where he renovated a massive country house on Shannon Run in Woodford County, turning it into a stunning mansion. Muwee wore handmade suits of silk ribbon. A braid of soft, fine shimmering blonde locks circled the top of her head. She sunbathed nude on the roof of their white columned manse and drove around in a vanilla-colored Cord convertible. Dear inherited her mother's flare, possessing that *je ne sais quoi* long before she met my grandfather.

Gene Bryant and Angelee Bradley were wildly attracted to each other from the moment they met. Both possessing innate charm, intelligence, and depth. Their courtship was passionate. Angelee first spotted Gene, who we called Daddy Gene, leaning against Solashin's Drugstore in downtown Lexington. Tall and gorgeous, lanky and lithe, Gene had one foot planted against the brick building, a cigarette dangled from his long musician fingers. Dear was in the passenger seat of her friend's convertible when the girl called out, "Hey Gene, I want to introduce you to Angelee Bradley." Dear ran a comb through her blonde curls as Gene approached in white pleated pants, white sweater, and a cocksure smile. After a few pleasantries, he asked if she would go out that night. Angelee said she already had a date. "Well break it," Gene smiled. Already smitten, my eighteen-year-old grandmother did just that.

Gene was the first-born son of Laura and Fred Bryant. Fred Bryant was a self-made man if there ever was one. Hailing from humble beginnings in a town called Quicksand in Breathitt County, Eastern Kentucky, his first job was as an electrician with a traveling circus. As a young man with an alcoholic father, Fred fought for a better life. He relocated his mother, brothers, and sisters to Lexington. Through hard work and sheer drive, he became a highly respected Shriner and community leader, responsible for the building of the Shriner's Hospital for Children in Lexington. His portrait hangs in the lobby today.

Fred also owned the Oldsmobile dealership in town. Gene used to take a shiny new car straight off his father's lot to pick up Angelee at her home on Shannon Run. They took long drives in the countryside through horse farms and rolling hills. When they found a place to pull over, they danced in the moonlight and made love under the stars.

Before long, Gene and Angelee were married with a baby on the way, my mother, Lynne. Daddy Gene had his own orchestra at the time which included preeminent musicians, Art Lund and Billy Butterfield. The band traveled extensively. Girls squealed for my handsome grandfather like they did for Frank Sinatra, even Billie Holiday approached him for a dance. Gene was a lady's man from the get-go, and eventually Angelee put her foot down, insisting her husband give up the life of a traveling music man. Gene acquiesced and went to work for his father's Oldsmobile dealership. As a show person myself, growing up, on and around the stage, I imagine it was a great disappointment and sacrifice for my grandfather to give up such an exciting path. By the same token, Angelee felt her own dreams bound, she dreamt of being a spy and flying an airplane, also being a professional writer. Like a racehorse that had been harnessed, she fought an identity solely characterized as a mother of four little children.

What appeared on the outside was a picture-perfect existence in a five-bedroom home on Fincastle Road in Lexington, overlooking the historic Henry Clay Estate. If you ask any of the four Bryant children, they will tell you it was an ideal childhood. Lynne, Bradley, Earl, and Leigh had tennis courts, a shuffleboard and swings in their backyard. Growing up they had little toy cars and toy horses in the front, along with a park across the street where they could play.

The Bryant's childhood Christmases on Fincastle Road in Lexington were like a scene out of a movie. On Christmas Eve, Daddy Gene would go to the downtown Oldsmobile garage and fill a truck with toys and gifts, then come home and cover the ceiling with balloons. He put snow on the Christmas tree, ate the cookies on the mantle and covered the living room with streamers and gifts. Then he went to the front door and rang the bells yelling, "Ho Ho Ho Merry Christmas!" Dear went around to wake the kids so they could hear Santa. Mamma gathered her younger brothers and sister to run down the steps and find a fairy land.

Aunt Leigh's most prominent memories of her childhood home are full of love and music. They performed plays, standing in a row in the living room, singing for their parents like the Family von Trapp. Daddy Gene taught them songs which they sang on the way to school and on the way to their house on Harrington Lake. We grandchildren learned those same songs as a rite of passage, "Heart of My Heart", "Glow Little Glow Worm", "I'm in Love with the Garbage Man's Daughter", "Little Sir Echo", and "School Days", to name a few.

That happiness Gene and Angelee experienced as young lovers was now overrun by a houseful of kids and mounting infidelity. "Woman killer!" Angelee screamed at the vacuum cleaner as she pushed it. Marital woes of the charismatic parents were kept largely out of sight from the four impeccably dressed children on Fincastle. My mother was old enough to see her parents struggle with the dissolution of their once passionate love. Mamma was a major factor in raising her younger siblings after Dear suffered what we now know is postpartum depression after Uncle Earl was born.

In the end, Gene was unfaithful one too many times and a fed-up Angelee pursued a flirtation of her own. Before the affair came to fruition, my grandfather had the phone tapped like any good military man might do and heard Angelee planning to meet a handsome, married surgeon in Cincinnati. Daddy Gene marched over to his house, dragged the doctor out in the country and beat him to a pulp. My teenage mother stood behind the wall and listened when the bloodied surgeon and his wife came to their door on Fincastle. "I don't blame you," the wife said to her husband. "She's so pretty, I could kiss her myself." The woman's graciousness regarding her spouse's planned infidelity put the whole sad situation in perspective. It also ended Dear's attempt to match Daddy Gene's infidelity.

I don't think my grandfather ever got over how he mishandled that relationship, squandering the love of an incredible woman, carelessly gambling and losing his home and life with his children. I remember Daddy Gene sitting silent and stoic, in a dark gray recliner, one long thin leg crossed over the other, cigarette still perpetually dangling from those beautiful hands. He spent his last decades facing a blaring television set in the small, dark living room of a house in the Zandale neighborhood of Lexington. A round table at his feet held a candy jar faithfully overflowing with tiny snickers, milky ways, and juicy fruit gum for us grandchildren. It was a far cry from their stately place on Fincastle. My great-grandfather Fred Bryant died peacefully at the ripe old age of eighty-three. Always the dutiful son, when his father passed away, Daddy Gene moved his mother, Laura Bryant, who we call Pommie, in with him and he lived out his years caring for her.

My big brother, Joseph Daniel "Chan" Chandler and I are the oldest of our cousins on the Bryant side and share in the memory of Daddy Gene being kind and loving but a little sad. We knew his younger brother, Earl Bryant, died of alcoholism at the age of thirty. We knew he was disappointed his marriage to Dear didn't last. Still, we hadn't an inkling how remarkable his life had been, leading him to that chair, smoking, deaf to everything, save his own melancholy surrender. By the time we were old enough to form an opinion, it seemed our grandfather was done.

Bluegrass Sons

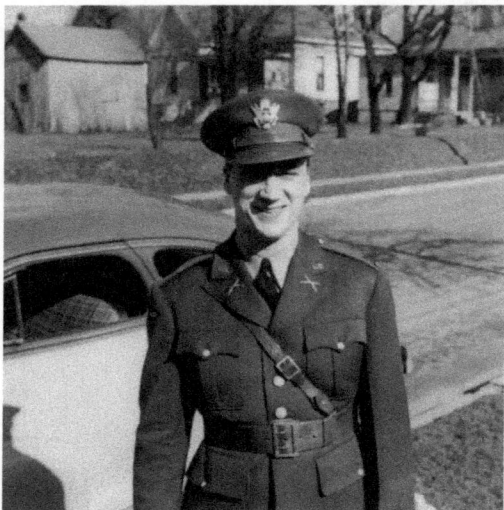

World War II Army Captain, Gene Bryant

Laura Bryant (front seat) with sons, Eugene and Earl Bryant, Gene's firstborn daughter, Lynne and her cousin, Earl's son Larry in Lexington, Kentucky.

CHAPTER
FOUR

The Indoctrination

Ithought Daddy Gene would be a good place to start in my attempt to unravel Uncle Brad's sense of duty and obedience to the military. "Dad was a Captain in the Army," Brad said. "I asked him a lot of questions when I could... when I got old enough to ask. He would occasionally talk about it but didn't really pursue it. He didn't make an issue about it and didn't try to discourage it."

It is unanimously agreed that the patriarch of the Bryant family was particularly tough on his firstborn son. Brad received the brunt of a brutishness I never witnessed from

Daddy Gene. "Daddy gave Brad hell," Mamma remembered sadly. At the same time, Bradley was Dear's heart, and she was fiercely protective over him. When he returned from the war, my grandfather possibly resented his beautiful son for being the new light of his wife's eye.

"He was tough," Uncle Brad readily acknowledges. "Very disciplined. He didn't… yeah, he was tough. I mean, I wouldn't say Dad was uh… probably he was tougher on me than anyone else. There's no question about it." He struggled with saying anything negative about his father but finally gave in with a laugh, "I remember as soon as he got back from the war, Dad took me to the barbershop and had all my hair cut off. I remember that. Because I'm so sweet!" My uncle joked in a baby voice, "I was too sweet!"

Mine is a family that does not talk bad about each other, or to each other, no matter what. There are things we have all done wrong, but as a general rule, it is not spoken of. Gene Bryant was a dichotomy. On one hand, he was an unfaithful, overly-strict disciplinarian who on occasion belittled his eldest. On the other, he was chief operator in creating the glorious memories of an extremely tight knit family. The Bryant siblings are deeply protective of each other. When a ten-year-old Earl came home bleeding, beaten by some kids in the neighborhood, Daddy Gene sent Brad right back out to defend his brother and confront the teenage assailants even though they were older and bigger than the son he sent out to battle.

"There was never any question about it," Uncle Brad told me matter of factly. "We were so close to our family, your mom, and Aunt Leigh, we were all so close. It just came naturally, frankly. If somebody was giving a family member a hard time, they had a problem. You know what I mean?"

When their close family split up, it was a difficult adjustment, for the youngest three especially. My mother had already married my father, a day after her twentieth birthday, and moved into the governor's mansion. Meanwhile, Daddy Gene lost their big, beautiful house on Fincastle, in arguably the nicest section of Lexington. He lost it due to gambling debts and his general mismanagement of life.

"I think with Dad," Brad explained, "he had an affair that caused him… it triggered the separation with mom, and he had to live with it. I think that's what it came down to," he let out a soft breath. "It was hard to believe… yep, yep. When they separated, it was really something." We sat silently for a moment, both knowing Daddy Gene never truly recovered.

Dear moved with Brad, Earl and Leigh to a smaller house in downtown Lexington on Forrest Avenue, or as Uncle Earl put it, Forrest Alley. My fourteen-year-old uncle was shocked and appalled to discover a real-life brothel across the street, complete with a wraparound New Orleans-style porch and flashing lights in the windows. This was a lifetime away from the mansion on Shannon Run where Angelee Bradley Bryant grew up, and a far cry from the idyllic house only a few miles away on Fincastle. Earl may have been disgruntled but my grandmother, now a divorced mother of four, was especially worried about her first-born son. "I was hanging around some kids who were characters," Uncle Brad admitted. This prompted Dear to reach out to the Sewanee Military Academy in Tennessee.

When I first heard this, a military academy seemed like an overly dramatic path for the liberal-minded family I knew, but upon further examination, it makes perfect sense. They offered Brad a scholarship to play football and Sewanee was one of the most prestigious military schools in the country in the 1960s. Rigorous in their training, it was tutelage in a battle-ready environment. Serving as a replacement for the free-thinking education in public school, the end goal was to prepare students to serve their country. If it was discipline Dear was looking for, she got more than she bargained for.

Brad thrived in Sewanee's world of order. He talks about the school now with such extreme fondness, warmth, and nostalgia. "Sewanee was definitely the beginning of all things military," Uncle Brad says confidently. "Sewanee was very focused, very driven. Focus on doing the right thing. You get up, you get out of bed, you know exactly what to do. You know how to make your bed, clean up, center, center, center, center. Get ready to go to class, come back from class. If you were an athlete, you go to practice. Everything was structured there was no… no flexibility from my standpoint whatsoever. It was a great place. Great place. Of course, it was in the middle of all the things going on, so the military was very much a passion all over the world, all over the United States."

United States military was indeed deeply focused in 1961. There was a lot going on. President John F. Kennedy was just beginning his term. The outgoing President Eisenhower warned the nation of our insatiable appetite for more and more weapons in a new military-crazed world. Eisenhower had the foresight to recognize if we were not vigilant, we would lose sight of striving for peace. Sewanee Military Academy was developed by men very much in step with the giant war machine. Over the years their headmasters included three legendary generals, Josiah Gorgas, Chief of Ordinance of the Confederacy, George R. Allin, Brigadier General of the United States Army and William R Smith, Superintendent at West Point Military Academy and Commander of the 36th Infantry Division in France during World War I. You can't tout these founding members without churning out soldiers who adhere to the same creed.

Racial tensions were out of control throughout the south when both of my uncles, Brad and Earl Bryant attended Sewanee. There were mobs, beatings, bombs and lynching at the hands of the Ku Klux Klan and those who protected them. The Freedom Riders left Washington D.C. on May 4th, 1961, to protest the failure of the southern states to uphold the rule outlawing segregation. Bravely, these civil rights activists and patriots put their safety and lives on the line to bring attention to states blatantly ignoring the Federal government. The violence inflicted upon anyone daring to challenge the racist south and their inhumane behavior toward the black population was unfathomable. It's hard to imagine those generals of Sewanee's past would have had the backs of any civil rights leader pushing peace.

"Erin, you know," said Uncle Earl who was captain of Sewanee's Sabre Drill Team, "Sewanee Military Academy, where Brad and I attended high school, was not some purely militaristic environment." He disagreed with my assessment of the school. My mom's brothers have deep sentimental attachments to their alma mater. "There were good teachers, good athletics," he continued. "We all attended church every Sunday. Sure, everyone had their designated duties, but it was not some hell hole pumping out badass soldiers."

Nonetheless, Sewanee did pump out a few badass risk takers. It was at the military academy that Brad met Andrew

Carter Thornton and the ensuing friendship changed the course of both their lives. As teenage boys, they found in each other a kindred spirit, each flourishing in the aggressively structured environment. Brad and Drew were different, but they complemented each other, the yin and yang of a perfect soldier. Nowadays, when Sewanee hits a sentimental chord with Brad, most of the nostalgia is wrapped around memories of his friend, Drew. "I met Drew right away at Sewanee and we hit it off, of course," Uncle Brad said with a smile palpable through the phone wires. "Drew and I were extremely close, almost like brothers. We became very, very good friends and it evolved from there. I mean Sewanee was a whole different world." It's been sixty years since they attended high school at the military academy but as Uncle Brad spoke about his old friend, it was clear to me they once had an unmistakable bond seldom formed in a person's lifetime.

Brad was there on a football scholarship, he always enjoyed sports and was very talented. Drew was astute but not an athlete. He was certainly capable but as my uncle put it, "Drew was just more of a character, I mean as far as living on the edge and taking chances." There was a water tower behind the school and Brad remembers Drew climbing the ladder to the very top and sitting up there by himself. When Sewanee authorities found out he was up there, they didn't know how to handle their rebel student. It caused a mighty ruckus back then, along with a present-day chuckle, "He was a character," Uncle Brad laughs. "But that's Drew, he was tough... living on the edge."

Brad's younger brother Earl was no fan of Drew's or their developing friendship. "What is interesting to me is how Drew Thornton is portrayed as some superbad dude,"

Uncle Earl remembers, irritated we're even discussing him. "At Sewanee, he appeared to be kind of a dumb ass, always just joking around. At halftime of a UK basketball game," he shook his head, "Drew and some other supposed karate guys were putting on an exhibition, breaking boards… Drew injected novocaine into his hands to desensitize them so hitting the boards wouldn't hurt. How dumb!"

While Earl Bryant was leery of Andrew Thornton, his big brother was irrevocably drawn to him. Brad and Drew bonded over their passion for physical fitness, a pension for discipline and mutual ideals of what it meant to protect this country. They found comfort, early on at least, in the government's dogma. I asked my mother, a trained and experienced psychotherapist, about this authoritarian persuasion that seemed readily installed in her brother and his friend. "It happens often with young men at that age," she said. "They want a cause."

The relationship that began as teenagers at a military academy led to a decidedly unorthodox business partnership. They became a kind of Butch Cassidy and the Sundance Kid, a pair of Robin Hoods crisscrossing the globe in perfect step with each other. Whether they were in step with Robin Hood's honorable creed of good versus evil, only Brad and Drew knew.

Long before Bradley Bryant became a mythical figure in Kentucky's criminal folklore, his first stop after high school at Sewanee was to protect America through the military. My family fighting for this country can be traced back to the Revolutionary War. My great-grandmother, Laura Bryant was proud of her membership in the DAR, the Daughters of the American Revolution. My great grandfather, Fred

Bryant's father, John Bryant, fought in the Civil War. Then came my grandfather, Gene Bryant and his brother Earl, both World War II veterans. Daddy Gene brought back guns from the war and took my uncles out to the dump and taught them how to shoot. When the time came, Gene's sons joined the service. Uncle Brad joined the Marines and Uncle Earl became a Captain in the Army, just like his father. In the Vietnam war, Earl was in charge of a company of medics, a MASH unit, then a clearing station, a smaller emergency care unit on the field.

Brad wanted to go to Vietnam while Earl was there. Dear would have had both sons in Vietnam, a terrible predicament for any parent. As fate would have it, she was dating a colonel who oversaw the reserves at the time. With the man's help, Dear was able to complicate Brad's efforts to be deployed to the Vietnamese jungle.

When Uncle Brad discusses his regimented life as a marine, active from 1966-1974, he becomes enthusiastic and energized. He accounts again in favorable terms how everything was structured, how each discipline was taught through physically rigorous training. Chief among all else, he tells me with pride, was "loyalty, loyalty, loyalty". As training progressed, he learned about weaponry, shooting and every type of defense you could imagine. Everything was based on a command, and "you always follow your commands". He became more knowledgeable as a soldier and admits that he was conditioned to always be aware of the purpose behind following that path. Uncle Brad emerged with a deeply rooted belief that everything he did, every movement, was infused with purpose. You didn't allow anything to interfere with your purpose. "You knew what you should or should not do," Brad explained. "There was never a question. It's complicated, but that's it."

I see the soldier he describes in the man I know today. Trained to defend against any enemy, trained to kill with his bare hands, was the sea in which he swam from the moment he joined the United States Marines. Mission. Discipline. Focus. Drive. God. Country. Flag. I find it sadly ironic that Dear's intention was to keep her son out of trouble when she enrolled Brad in the military academy in the woods of Tennessee. How could she have ever guessed it would burn such a sinister path.

Bradley Bryant (top) and Drew Thornton (bottom)
at the Sewanee Military Academy, 1962

CHAPTER
FIVE

A Motel off I-75

Bradley Fred Bryant was only twenty-five years old when his buddy from Sewanee, Andrew Carter Thornton, drove him the hour and a half from Lexington to a motel outside of Cincinnati. Thus began a journey mired in the quicksand of fighting endless corruption around the globe.

"When I was in Philadelphia," Brad spoke of this introduction, "Drew had come to visit me several times and I had gone down to see him." They kept in touch, visiting each other between Philadelphia and their hometown, Lexington, Kentucky, always interested in what the other was doing.

"He had gotten involved in some things... going through some situations. He ended up talking me into going to meet some people in Cincinnati with him."

Drew did not come right out and say they were CIA agents they were going to meet. He didn't tell Brad who he was working for at that point. There were just some people he wanted him to meet on the Kentucky-Ohio border. Now there was a situation that was complicated, but Drew didn't elaborate beyond that.

During our recorded conversations about his past, I quickly realized my uncle would speak in non-specific terms. It would always be a situation, a certain issue, or a complicated thing. I usually got the point but had to read between the lines. Brad is at his core a secret keeper, a team player, not a snitch. His orders and code of ethics are deeply ingrained. If I pushed too hard, he would shut me down in an instant. While loving him dearly, I know him well enough to be a little bit scared.

I did gather in no uncertain terms that Brad and Drew had an embedded understanding of the concept of duty. Still, there was never any pressure between the two men. They made individual decisions about what kind of activity each would engage. There was an embedded sense of respect and boundaries as they honored the other's path and choices. Brad and Drew would share opinions on a subject or task at hand but ultimately, it was up to each man regarding what he would or would not do.

On that smoldering summer afternoon in 1969, Brad and Drew arrived at a small motel off I-75 where two agents in casual business attire awaited. They had set up a table in the middle of a drab room next to an air conditioner for their young guests, a former Marine and a former Army paratrooper. They had a proposition for the well-trained Kentucky boys. It was natural for the agents to assume they were all on the same team. Mission. Discipline. Focus. Drive. God. Country. Flag. The CIA is famous for convincing young soldiers to accept audacious directions and there was no reason for them to assume they would be met with anything but respect from Brad and Drew.

Douglas Valentine, author of *The CIA as Organized Crime: How Illegal Operations Corrupt America and the World* and *Strength of the Pack* writes about the line between crime and law enforcement, "What I learned is there isn't a line." Valentine talks about a sweet spot around 1968, after World War II, the good war, and before the full repercussions of Vietnam, the bad war, were realized. It was a time when most military-minded adult males viewed themselves as the ones who saved the world for democracy. The very moment in history Valentine wrote about is when Brad and Drew met with CIA agents at that lonely motel off the interstate.

Uncle Brad said the men who beckoned him to the clandestine meeting were light spoken, straight forward, "Kind of uh… tough." There wasn't a lot of conversation, not a lot of small talk. They were in their early thirties and wore suits, "nothing fancy, basic stuff." Drew was already in on the deal, already working for the mysterious gentlemen before leading Brad toward this day that changed his life.

There were things going on in Lexington at the University of Kentucky and the men in the motel wanted to gather information. The foundation was drugs. At this juncture, Brad didn't have any dealings with the drug-taking population. He was strait-laced, athletic, and meticulous as to what he put in his body. They discussed a plan for Brad and Drew to go undercover. I use this rudimentary term for what my uncle described as interaction.

"They wanted interaction," Uncle Brad reported. "Drew was more... let's just say he was more compatible with that type of environment. Some of the people he'd fit in better with than I would. You had to be a player, so to speak. Drew was more open to that stuff than I was. Let's say he would blend in better."

The two found their way organically as undercover agents. Given their extensive training, it's not surprising their roles emerged effortlessly. Brad was disciplined, dependable and laser-focused. He was also blessed with the extraordinary good looks most of my family on the Bryant side have, high cheekbones and perfect bone structure thanks to a splash of Shawnee blood. Drew was the dark horse, the charmer, the bad boy with an appetite for drugs and women. Drew drank heavily with the men and seduced the ladies. He was the guy who sat at a table with the rest of the players snorting lines of cocaine, putting people at ease with a devil-may-care personality. Drew had also just gotten out of law school and taken up with the police force, becoming part of the first DEA team in Lexington.

Those tough, suited gents who summoned Brad and Drew to the motel were not oblivious to the fact that both young men had deep Kentucky connections across the board. Bradley Bryant came with familial ties to both Lexington's high society and the Las Vegas crowd they would soon task him to find out about. This gave Brad access not many had. The agents had Brad and Drew's number long before they put forth their agenda. The handlers knew they were dealing with a dedicated, fearless Marine who this paratrooper, turned cop, turned CIA contractor, trusted with his life. They all spoke the same language.

"So, the men in the motel, they spoke your language, right?" I asked Uncle Brad. "They spoke a language you understood?"

"Oh yeah. Basically, yes. Oh yeah," Brad said squarely. "We didn't go out with any doubt in our mind of what we were thinking about. We just had to make some decisions. It was complicated but we had to make a decision. Steps had to be taken. Very methodical steps had to be taken… it was interesting."

Lexington Artist Henry Faulkner and Anita Madden
Photo by Frank Anderson

CHAPTER
SIX

Midnight in the Garden of Good & Evil

Graddy Johnson's family has been in Lexington, Kentucky since 1780, their farmhouse is one of the oldest in the state. A lifelong friendship with the flamboyant horse breeders, Preston and Anita Madden granted Graddy full access at a very early age to a gilded and cloistered world. As a popular bartender near the University of Kentucky, he was exposed to every angle of the city including the larger-than-life personalities who made up the darker corners.

"It's very cliquish," Graddy said of his hometown. "It's corrupt, it's elegant, it's bloody. It's drunk. I like a line from

Midnight in the Garden of Good and Evil, 'Lexington's like a beautiful woman with mud on her face.' You wouldn't believe some of the things you walk in to. If you've got the inside track, it's unlike any place in the world."

Today, Lexington has gone through a massive transformation. Just as Miami is not the Miami of the sixties, and Malibu is not the Malibu of the eighties, Lexington is not the Lexington of the seventies. With continual growth and expansion, nowadays most cities resemble each other, whitewashed into an everyplace for everybody. But in the nineteen-seventies and eighties, Lexington was not a particularly easy place to blend in. It's no wonder the feds picked these two young guns to infiltrate the scene. Brad and Drew were as connected as they were rebellious, slick, and trained as they were green.

The drug culture had run rampant, it's no wonder authorities tried to get a handle on it. It was wild all over the United States. The whole country was feeling the cold death of the sixties and its peaceful idealism after recent assassinations of three iconic civil rights leaders, President John F. Kennedy, Martin Luther King Jr., and Bobby Kennedy. Nixon was president, Vietnam was still raging, and the anti-war protesters and their love crusade were out in full force. The CIA knew full well Bradley Bryant was not of that persuasion. He was a young man who had in fact pledged allegiance to the antithesis of the peace movement blanketing the country.

"Anti-war protesters?" Uncle Brad demanded sharply when I broached the subject. "No, we wouldn't tolerate any of that. We were definitely disciplined to… no that was not part of it. That wouldn't go very far. Oh yeah, there was never any question about that. I don't know why but it was the way we grew up. Very, very disciplined in that area. We didn't have much compassion for anybody that would demonstrate against the country or anything like that."

I picture Brad at this moment of American history, straight-backed and bewildered at the loosening of an entire society. Acid-rocking, cross-dressing, Alice Cooper had recently popped up while simultaneously the overtly sexual Donna Summer, with her moans and syncopated beats, ruled the airwaves. This booze and drug fomented manic energy trickled down around the University of Kentucky's campus and magnified at the Library Lounge, a place already under investigation. They used Brad's connections to penetrate the scene, knowing his brother-in-law, my father, Dan Chandler, was a good friend of the club's owner.

Jimmy Lambert was sandy-haired and rail-thin. He looked like Steve McQueen in his giant aviator sunglasses inside the dark bar. A permanent grin reeked rock-n-roll bad boy. He provided stiff drinks and great music for doctors, politicians, and college students. The CIA was looking to infiltrate the drug scene in Lexington and Jimmy was in the thick of it. He not only owned the Library Lounge but had nightly parties at his riverfront home, a glamorous go-to spot for the country club and horsey set. It was a hideaway for Lexington's movers and shakers with piles of cocaine in every corner and prostitutes at the ready. No rules seemed to apply to this lucky bunch of so and so's.

"What was Jimmy Lambert's connection to the CIA probe?" I asked Uncle Brad.

"Jimmy was a resource," he stated flatly.

"Jimmy was a resource because he did drugs and had a popular nightclub?"

"Right. That's it," he said. "No big deal. Nothing beyond that."

I was seven years old in 1972 and remember clearly being propped up in a red leather barstool in the Library Lounge next to my father. The place was empty, and Jimmy stood behind the bar. He seemed like a movie star. I had the same shy reaction when I met Burt Reynolds that same year. These were snazzy dudes. Jimmy and Daddy were laughing about who knows what. It looked like a living room strangely placed in the middle of a small strip mall a few blocks from the University of Kentucky campus. Slightly nefarious, with neon accents, it was decorated in velvet and leather maroons, eerily similar to the Caesar's Palace atmosphere my father would soon take over at the other end of the country. Daddy bridged the gap between Vegas and Lexington in a way the two decadent cities had never been bridged before.

I called Mr. Lambert, now in his eighties, to discuss the times. "I always loved your dad," Jimmy said. "There wasn't one person that didn't absolutely love your dad. He would light up a room with his quotes and everything you know. You're from a great family that goes way back."

Jimmy Lambert was sentimental like so many Kentuckians about my grandfather, Happy Chandler, who in 1935 was Kentucky's youngest governor. After serving as the second only Baseball Commissioner from 1945-1951, he was elected for a second term as governor twenty years later in 1955. Pappy traveled to every town and holler for over sixty years, shaking hands and singing on the campaign trail. He sang his heart out for nearly a century. Everyone around here remembers my ninety-year-old grandfather at Rupp Arena during a special Kentucky Wildcats basketball game standing in the middle of the court surrounded by swaying cheerleaders and tearful ball players, belting out "My Old Kentucky Home" like a rock star.

"I remember I was about ten years old," Lambert reflected in a warm, gravelly voice, "Happy Chandler down in Harrison Kentucky, 'Happy Days Are Here Again' and all of that." Then my elderly friend said suddenly, unexpectedly, "I love you. Anybody named Chandler, just count me in."

During our conversation, I delicately approached the seventies in Lexington, the scene he and my father were so much a part of. I didn't see any need to mention to Mr. Lambert, safely down on the Florida coast, just awakened from his nap, about drug charges, the trial, or his years in prison. I wanted to spare him another reminder of those long-ago headlines in every newspaper dragging him through the mud. My goal was purely to touch base and speak to a friend who was there at that time and who, like my uncle, father and brother, had also been carelessly speculated and inaccurately written about over the years.

I reminded Mr. Lambert of the time my thirty-something father failed to report a proper tax return. When the governor's son spent three months in a Louisville lockdown for the white-collar crime, Dan Chandler's buddy Jimmy Lambert sent him a steak dinner every single night for three months. "That's right, I did," Jimmy laughed. "I forgot about that. I sure did."

It must have been extraordinary to have such an ally in that unapologetic land of excess. There was something of the roaring twenties in Lexington in the 1970s. Jimmy Lambert had a leading role in the cast of interesting characters with an attitude of untouchability. With his popular nightclub, the Studio 54 of Lexington, plus a secluded home down by the river, Jimmy provided a glamorous space for Lexingtonians to live out their wildest fantasies. Of course, such blatant libertines created negative attention and made Jimmy Lambert a plausible scapegoat for law enforcement.

Nine full years after Brad and Drew met in that Cincinnati motel room tasked to investigate the local drug culture, Lexington's wild party came to an abrupt halt... or at least a melancholic pause. On January 20th, 1984, The *New York Times* headline screamed, **GRAND JURY IN DRUG INQUIRY NAMES LEADING KENTUCKIANS**. The *Lexington Herald-Leader* splashed on their front page the same day, **Lambert, Anita Madden Indicted: Club Owner, Horsewoman Among 5 Charged in Probe**. The Grand Jury charged forty-four-year-old Jimmy Lambert with fifty-nine counts of possession or distribution of cocaine, marijuana, or methaqualone, one count of conspiracy to distribute cocaine and one count of violating federal firearms laws. Ed Bean wrote in the *Herald-Leader*:

> Lexington Nightclub owner James P. Lambert delivered an impromptu monologue. Rumored last summer to have fled the country, a confident and sardonic Lambert wearing cowboy boots, jeans and a hat that advertised Red Man chewing tobacco, joked with reporters about the investigation and needled federal prosecutors as they passed by, "I'm going to ask him to play the bedroom tapes for you."

Gary Cohn and Michael York of the *Lexington Herald-Leader* uncovered an attempted police sting in 1981. They wrote about Jimmy's reverse-sting when he recorded a police informant at his home, the infamous party house on Old Dobbin Road in Lexington. "There's a lot of people out there that say you're the heavyweight," a man is heard on the recording before pressing Jimmy to "move some product."

"I don't buy coke," Lambert's recorded voice replies. "I don't sell coke. You could not come up with one person I have sold one drug to in my entire life, and I can pass a polygraph on that. Maybe I live too nice or got too many broads. The only people that think I got anything to do with cocaine are cops. My heart is pure," Lambert quotes Sir Lancelot, "therefore, I am unafraid."

Jimmy Lambert spent the next three years in prison.

"My unshakable belief that justice prevails in the U.S.A," Anita Madden stated indignantly, "has been severely shaken by this grossly unfair indictment by the federal grand jury." Anita was charged with conspiring to obstruct justice in her friend Jimmy Lambert's probe. She was accused of the illegal disclosure of secret grand jury testimony by way of a court reporter slipping her carbon copies of some one hundred pages of court documents.

Anita Cannon Myers Madden was the most dazzling and misunderstood of the bunch conservative authorities attempted to shame. Born in Eastern Kentucky, Anita became queen of horse country when she married Preston West Madden, heir to Hamburg, a historic and respected thoroughbred breeding farm. His grandfather, John E. Madden, "The Wizard of the Turf," purchased Hamburg Place in 1898. Preston carried his southern gothic heritage like a noose around his black turtleneck. Both Preston's father and uncle committed suicide, leaving his brother Patrick and him millions of dollars and a dark pall over their horse farm. When the striking heir, in his uniform of sleek charcoal suits and dark glasses, married the wild, blonde goddess from the mountains known to the University of Kentucky football team as the 'Palomino,' they became instant legends. Tennessee Williams could not have conjured a more glamorous pair.

Hamburg produced five Derby winners, five Preakness Stakes winners and the first Triple Crown winner, Sir Barton. Much of this success was due to Anita, an incredibly smart and capable horse breeder and businesswoman to be reckoned with.

"I put her on the racing commission, if you remember," Governor John Y. Brown reminded me during our conversation shortly before his death. "I was going to make her chairman. But I already had Bill Sturgill who was in my Department of Energy as Cabinet Secretary. I liked Anita." John Y. was one of Jimmy Lambert's best friends and another key ingredient in the stew of diamond-studded personalities.

Anita was more like the entertainers I grew up with in Las Vegas than other ladies of privilege in Kentucky. She was a woman after my own theatrical heart. Seeming most comfortable in costumes of velvet and suede, silk, and feathers, Anita's best friend was Suzy DeKeyser, Las Vegas boutique owner of Suzy Creamcheese at the Aladdin Hotel. Chan and I lived in a suite right off the swimming pool at the Aladdin during our dad's stint as casino host there. I perused the treasures filling the clothes racks of Suzy Creamcheese regularly, and later Hot Cha Cha at Caesar's, dropping countless hundreds for my own costumes. Casino boutiques and their shop girls served as another form of babysitting, so when I paged my father he faithfully showed up, often with his buddy Lee Chagra, to buy my doe skin, beaded flare jeans and suede halters with feathers. Only now does Daddy's ever-present wad of cash seem suspicious.

These stage worthy styles were more age appropriate for Anita Madden and had a hand in turning her into a poster child for that scintillating moment in time. Her friends flew back and forth in a private jet between the Lexington Bluegrass and Las Vegas McCarran International airports. The like-minded revelers were another straw, another rolled up hundred-dollar bill, between Kentucky and Vegas.

Ironically, or perhaps by design, Anita is best known for her world-renowned bacchanalian Derby Eve parties. Her colossal galas rivaled that of the Egyptians. Preston and Anita decorated their home in a fashion Larry Flynt would find appropriate. There was melodramatic furniture in every room befitting a gaudy palace. Life-size original Renaissance paintings encased in massive gold frames which overshadowed the art itself.

My family adored the eccentric pair. My grandfather was particularly fond of Anita. Mammy and Pappy both recognized the sincerity of this striking woman. My mother and father followed suit. My brother, Chan, felt the warmth and welcome in Anita's eyes, signaling with every glance that he was on the inside. I felt the same inclusion. We both appreciated a soft place to land in the Bluegrass when we were struggling with our broken family. Forced to shuffle between our father's adopted life in Las Vegas and our mother's in Texas, Anita's Kentucky home provided unconditional acceptance when houses of more 'respectable' Lexingtonians did not. We all recognized, despite the show they put on, they were atypically real. The parties, the wealth, the extravagance on display did not sully the raw humanity exuding from the couple. Their depth of experience and mountain of pain was palpable, right alongside their acknowledgment and appreciation of blessings bestowed. The intention to ride them out as high and long as granted seemed their birthright.

This woman who radiated from the pinnacle of over-the-top decadence told Lexington newscaster Sue Wiley, "If I am reincarnated, I want to come back as Dan Chandler," Anita said. "Because he has more fun than anybody I've ever known."

"She was just as sweet as she could be," my mother says now. "Of course, I liked the fact she loved your Daddy so much." Still, Mamma remembers with sadness, Anita dancing wildly in the middle of a circle of people while Preston watched on stoically, expressionless, before turning and walking away. This, in my mother's romantic eyes, was completely tragic. She never liked the Lexington social scene in the sixties and seventies, wild with alcohol and wife swapping. It was foreign to her. With all of Gene and Angelee Bryant's problems, they never took to the streets with their very souls.

There was a house on the Madden's farm, behind the main mansion, it was an octagon-shaped place with screens all around. Mamma recalls the atmosphere as ominous, like a tropical scene from Somerset Maugham's *Miss Sadie Thompson*. Anita was in a silk robe and boa, lounging on a chaise while several tiny dogs crawled all over, licking her face. Daddy discussed a racehorse with Preston who stood against a giant stone fireplace, cigarillo in hand, saying, "Presto don't gotta do nothin'."

The Maddens lived like characters in a novel of their own making. It was all there, the southern gothic mansion, the thoroughbreds, the gorgeous black German Shepherds, the towering oak trees down the long gravel drive. The placement of their very bodies in a room was theatrical, languid, and intentional. Whatever dramatics and motivations therein, these two had a passion for flare.

Erin Chandler

CHAPTER
SEVEN

Cocaine Bear

As holds true to most rumors, there are accuracies to be found. Reports of bad cops in Kentucky in the 70s and 80s were founded. In fact, we had dirty cops on tap. Bill Canan was a notoriously shady character and the disappearance and apparent murders of two beautiful, young college women were inexplicably connected to him. When those girls vanished, any fool could see there was foul play.

There was a dark pall swirling around the state's capital during that time and many Kentucky government workers and police officers were locked up in quick succession, accused of murder or conspiracy to commit murder, drug planting, drug dealing and other salacious crimes. Uncle Brad's buddy Drew Thornton kept dangerous company and many of them were part of the Lexington, Kentucky police force.

I am reminded of what Nelson Brickham, the CIA officer who created the Phoenix program during the Vietnam War era told Douglas Valentine for his book *The CIA as Organized Crime: How Illegal Operations Corrupt America and the World*, "I have described the Intelligence Service as a socially acceptable way of expressing criminal tendencies. A guy who has strong criminal tendencies but is too much of a coward to be one would wind up in a place like the CIA if he had the education… mercenaries who found a socially acceptable way of doing these things and I might add getting very well paid for it."

The best-selling author was kind enough to impart his hard earned and researched knowledge to me over a recorded Zoom conversation. Valentine talks about his own schooling in the police world, how his father taught him to see behind the costume. "Most people don't see the cops associating with professional criminals and making money in the process," Valentine said. "They believe that when a guy puts on a uniform, the guy who was a bully in school and didn't develop the skills to be a plumber or go to college, he becomes virtuous. But the guys who go into law enforcement relate more to the crooks they associate with on a daily basis, than the citizens they're supposed to protect and serve. They're corrupted."

Melanie Flynn was twenty-four years old when she went missing. The daughter of a Kentucky state senator was a singer with such high aspirations she changed her name and moved to the big city. Melanie rode horses professionally before a riding accident caused her a lengthy hospital stay and permanent damage to her sense of taste and smell. She was just a baby searching for her next move when she hooked up with Bill Canan, a good friend and associate of Drew Thornton. It was a careless calculation that cost Melanie her life. She did not survive the year she went undercover with Canan. Smitten with the short, stocky policeman, she agreed to introduce him to her drug–taking buddies as her boyfriend so he could slip into the scene unchecked.

"He was an intimidating guy," a Lexington graphic designer commented. "He always had an air of danger around him." She recalled the aggressive dark-haired cop with a 'handlebar' mustache, brandishing guns and snorting enormous amounts of cocaine. She never saw him sober, always drinking heavily. Bill was part of the regular crowd at a local bar called Outside Inn Again, and another bar across the street on Lane Allen Rd called, Friends & Company. Several of the shadier cops were regulars at both watering holes. "He was a scary dude," she said, "these people were not fooling around."

A cop hopped up on cocaine, showing off a loaded gun and groping my friend is an unpleasant image but not hard to reach. Growing up in a casino in Las Vegas every summer from the age of seven, I have dined with hundreds of men like Canan. I have spent countless days on boats and evenings in fancy restaurants with Canans licking their chops at the latest business opportunity, gambling coup or waitress. I have witnessed how they see women, how they treat them, how they use them. I shudder to think of how little the men I am familiar with would care about Melanie Flynn, how little they indeed cared about the steady stream of Melanie Flynns in their lives. Maybe that was the case with Bill Canan, maybe it was the same with Drew Thornton. I would bet my life that her life was of little consequence to any of them.

What is indisputable is that girls like Melanie don't just disappear. They try to become famous and move to big cities or stay home and marry someone rich. Sometimes they never marry and die tragically alone of drug overdoses after multiple attempts at Alcoholics Anonymous. One thing I am sure of is women of her ilk crave attention and don't vanish into thin air at twenty-four years old.

"Who was Bill Canan?" I asked Uncle Brad.

"Canan was a close friend of Drew's," he answered without hesitation.

"Was he a friend of yours?"

"I knew Bill, I didn't have a relationship with him. I knew him," Brad said. "I didn't agree, frankly, with some things they were doing… things Canan was involved with. But that was okay, no big deal. I really wasn't into it, but I just didn't get involved with Bill. I had my own… I kept everything separate."

I asked Uncle Brad about Henry Vance, Chief Administrative Officer to former Kentucky Governor Julian Carroll. "He wasn't anything," Uncle Brad sluffed the question off. "Just a guy that knew some people." Vance also went to prison, reported to have been involved in a murder for hire.

"Was Drew close to him?" I asked.

"Drew knew him," Brad said.

I asked my uncle about Melanie Flynn and her disappearance. "Melanie Flynn…" I pressed for any insight into the forty-year-old mystery, "I guess she was dating Canan? Did that have anything to do with the drug trafficking stuff?"

"No. No," Brad said. "I just think it was a relationship… apparently, I guess it went wrong."

"That's an understatement," I said under my breath.

"I don't know," Uncle Brad countered flatly. "And I didn't know. They actually… when I was on vacation…" referring to his decade in federal prison, "they came down and tried to interview me about that. Of course, I didn't know anything, so I just didn't talk to them."

Bradley Bryant and his beautiful wife

CHAPTER
EIGHT

The Good Shephard

When I was little, Uncle Brad lived in Philadelphia. I remember visiting their magnificent home during Easter. The giant red brick mansion had an endless back yard with a creek surrounding their pristinely manicured estate. One of my favorite pictures with Chan was taken there. I have on a long patchwork dress and wildflowers in my copper-colored hair. Chan is wearing a brown suit, looking like Donny Osmond with his thick head of rich brown locks. You see us from behind, we're carrying Easter baskets. My brother has one arm around my shoulders, the other points to more painted eggs. As a child, I never questioned where Uncle Brad's giant amount of wealth came from. I never thought about why my cousins lived in that enormous house in Pennsylvania instead of Kentucky. Details trickled out over the years about a waste company and how it started with a felonious character named Biff, then how a different clean-up operation called Bryson emerged with my other uncles, Earl Bryant and Joel Stevenson. I remember a fire destroyed that big mansion a few years after that Easter picture was taken.

Now I realize that when we visited him in Philadelphia, it was the exact time in Brad's life that his relationship with Sewanee buddy Drew Thornton was morphing into a full-fledged adult partnership. Drew had been to law school, and he was a police officer on Lexington's first narcotics squad. Brad was busy running a successful waste company in Pennsylvania. They were in perfect sync with each other while simultaneously living very different lives.

I asked Uncle Brad how he came to be a respected businessman in Philadelphia. "I got involved with this guy in New York," he explained. The guy was Biff Halloran who he met through a mutual friend. Biff was looking for someone he could trust to run his family's business in waste control. He asked Brad to move up to Philadelphia.

"Was he involved in any kind of mafia situation?" I asked, remembering Biff Halloran from my childhood.

"Biff? Yes, "Brad confirmed. "I would say Biff probably was. He had a lot of contacts like that. And it ended up getting him killed, eventually." An image came into my head of a sniveling Biff in a warehouse full of goons. He begs for his life like we see time and again in mafia movies, making up excuses for his loose lips or skimming money, whatever it was that made the boss order his demise. I asked how it happened.

"Well, I don't know specifically, but he ended up disappearing, years later. He was just road trash." Road trash is a sentiment Uncle Brad repeats a lot. A definitive statement leaving nothing to the imagination about what he thinks of a person.

I met Biff when I was a little girl living on Elm Street in Versailles, Kentucky. What comes to mind is a beefy, blonde figure at our front door. My father was a man's man, a guy's guy who grew up in boarding schools like The Little Outfit in Arizona and Darlington in Rome, Georgia. Daddy followed that up with years in college sports, playing for the University of Kentucky on Adolph Rupp's undefeated basketball team. These testosterone-fueled experiences taught him to get along with every male personality imaginable and he was never discriminant about bringing shady characters into our orbit. With a potentially lucrative deal on the table, boundaries were disregarded, and everybody felt at home. One day Biff let himself into ours.

"Hey Honey? Baby?" I heard Biff call out. "Sugar, where's Danny boy?" A bloated, scarred face under a tight ring of pale, sweaty curls peered into the foyer. Stepping boldly onto the black and white tiles at the bottom of the steps, he looked up, "Sugar!? Honey!? Sweetie?" He called my beautiful twenty-something mother these names repeatedly and all in a row. Biff was a gropey football coach type. Not to insult coaches, I have met some of the greats, but he was the kind who might have stumbled into the profession because of size, a loud voice and the inability to do anything else. In my fifty-plus-year history with this type of man, I chalk Biff Halloran up to the first letch I came in contact with.

Biff was once the brother-in-law of Daddy's long-time girlfriend, Delores. It suddenly dawns on me for the first time that perhaps my Uncle Brad knew Delores and Biff before Daddy did. "Did you introduce Daddy to Delores?" I asked about the mother of my half-sister, Happy.

"I may have, I may have. I don't remember, I may have," Uncle Brad said, only a touch suspiciously. Then he laughed, thinking about Delores, "your dad had his hands full."

Daddy cavorted with people from both sides of the bench, both sides of the aisle and both sides of the law. I wondered where Biff and his family fit in. I wondered if the waste company was on the up and up.

"It was an up and up company," Brad said when I asked. "Biff's father was a very successful businessman in Philadelphia and a contractor. He had a major contracting company up there. I moved up there to take over the company, run the company, which was a company that collected waste material. It was a gradual process. I got involved with his company and learned the ABC's. At that point it was all shovels and backbone. It was all construction. Everything was by hand, very labor intensive. I got some knowledge about a company that was a Vacall service. Vacall vacuum trucks that collected this stuff and we would dump it in our recycling bin, and we would clean it. We would collect it as different types of crushing materials, crush it into certain sizes and it would be applicable for tracks, cinder blocks, you name it."

It turns out Biff and his dad were not on good terms. The elder Halloran put more faith in Bradley Bryant than his own son. Uncle Brad learned the waste business from top to bottom. When it eventually came to pass that Biff was indeed a bad actor and siphoning money from the company, basically, "not a good person," as my uncle put it, he took the knowledge gained and branched out on his own

"I started a new company, not with Biff, but with your Uncle Earl and Uncle Joel," Brad explains the company's evolution from a Halloran family business to a Bryant family business. Going into business with his brother, Earl Bryant and brother-in-law, Joel Stevenson, he knew he would be working with people he could trust. The three formed a company of their own doing the same thing but more efficiently. Uncle Earl developed a piece of equipment, a truck-mounted vacuum service, which they patented. The Bryant brothers and their brother-in-law, Joel, built a successful company that worked with U.S. Steel and several oil companies. They worked with a steel company in Idaho, a steel company in Pittsburgh and another in Alabama. The more developed they became, the more doors would open all over the United States.

Joel Stevenson, Brad and Earl's little sister Leigh's husband, was focused, driven and ambitious. When Uncle Joel started working in the waste business, he wasn't sure what his professional future would look like. Joel had been drafted by the Cleveland Browns to play professional football but thirty-five pounds underweight and fresh from the service, he was too tired to give it his all. I'm not certain if it's a pang of regret I hear when he talks of never giving his professional sports career a good shot. Although, it's clear as day how he felt when Brad offered him this new opportunity. Joel was ready to put it all out on the field.

"When I got to Philadelphia," Joel said, "I put my nose to the grindstone. I went to work. I said I'm gonna learn this business. He's given me an opportunity now and that's what I'm going to do. I went to work learning the business. It was very, very challenging and something that I really liked. I was fortunate that I had two brothers-in-law, Bradley and Earl, that I liked and I think they respected me."

Joel and Earl worked sixteen hours a day, five days a week, eight hours on Saturday and Sunday for ninety days. They went into schools and businesses that had coal dust and proceeded to clean and recycle it. From the ground up, deep in the bowels of wherever they had to do this cleaning, they learned the business. Along with Bradley, Joel gives credit to the timing of the venture, saying they were at the right place, at the right time, with the right thing. Uncle Brad is credited by both of his partners as the visionary, the idea man, and president of Bryson Corporation. He knew the business, pulled ash out of the flus in schools when they burned coal. The earlier, less efficient way of cleaning had been to shovel the ash in buckets and run it up to the dump truck. "Well, that was a bunch of baloney," Joel said. Brad got a vacuum truck that cut that down, requiring less people, as well as taking less time. This of course equaled more money.

Only now is my family aware that Brad was involved with people and things light years away from the waste company. I asked my aunt and uncles, whose financial lives and careers depended on Brad at the time, if they saw anything suspicious. Did they suspect something might be transpiring other than their hazardous waste business? Did they ever imagine Uncle Brad was working for the government… or a drug lord from El Paso?

"I didn't see any of it," my mom's younger sister, Aunt Leigh remembers. "We had no clue. Nothing. Earl didn't know about it. Joel didn't know. He kept that whole side of his life, that we now know was happening, he kept that completely separate from their business. I think he was trying to protect all of us, of course."

Joel was aware Brad had different business interests having to do with hazardous waste including the International Harvester Dealership in Savannah. He realized his brother-in-law, who he saw as a visionary had four or five different scenarios going on in regard to hazardous waste. "Bradley Bryant is the best entrepreneur I have ever known," Uncle Joel told me. "I teach entrepreneurship at the University of South Carolina and have for twenty years. Bradley Bryant is the best."

It was clear beyond a shadow of a doubt that Joel had great respect for Brad. What I wanted to know, and not so delicately probed, was how he felt when these other activities were brought to light. What did strait-laced, conservative, law-abiding Joel Stevenson think about Bradley Bryant's secret agent status and simultaneous life in Las Vegas with my father working as militarized security for Jimmy Chagra? Still deeper, when did he find out Brad was smuggling drugs from Colombia to Lexington?

"When did I find out?" Uncle Joel asked loudly, defensively. "I don't even remember finding out. Earl and I worked with Bradley for three or four years, okay? We had a three-bedroom apartment in Birmingham and one of the bedrooms was the office. Leigh was our executive secretary. Bradley was in Philadelphia. I mean we didn't see him at all. Not very often anyway. He's always going and doing and going and doing and going and doing. But we were in business by God! The other people that you're mentioning... I'm giving you some background, so you'll have some idea why I'm... you know... is he walking around in a fog? Is he not paying attention? You dad gum I wadn't paying attention to a Jimmy Chagra or Biff or Drew! I didn't have time to do that!"

CHAPTER
NINE

The Company

"The Company" became a legendary dog whistle, folklore in the drug trafficking rumor mill. This menacing name is bandied about in Domonic Dunne's *Power, Privilege and Justice*, a true-crime docuseries, *The Fall of an International Drug Trafficker: Dangerous Company*, and the ill-informed *The Bluegrass Conspiracy*. Reporter Sally Denton ominously describes Brad Bryant and Andrew Thornton like characters from some dark forest of murderous, drug trafficking socialites. In truth, the only company Brad and Drew had together was a security detail they temporarily formed called Executive Protective Services. This was a side hustle born of a need to gather information for the CIA.

With intel gained from my own faulty wires, I asked my uncle a question I thought legitimate at the time, "When did you and Drew form The Company?"

"We never talked about it like that," Brad replied sharply. "No one ever knew what we were doing, okay? Drew and I were partners. We did everything together. Our decisions were made together." He explained his undercover work with Drew and the fact that there was no "Company," they never referred to themselves as such. Any clandestine work was concentrated between the two men, there was not a wide swath of criminals they exposed some master plan to. "We discussed things and did everything in confidence together, but we never asked about who we were working for... who we were working with. Together we would talk about things, but nowhere else. We never had any other conversations ever with anybody else."

The journalistic tragedy is that reporters, reputable and hacks alike, have talked about this non-existent organization for decades. You can pull up any number of false reports by conspiracy theorists and FBI special agents all presenting as truth their take on The Company and inevitably the first names mentioned, the so-called 'master minds' of the operation, are Brad Bryant and Drew Thornton. To be clear, at long last, there was no such enterprise.

Over the years, as people in all walks of life do, Brad and Drew formed individual connections. As Brad ran a waste company in Philadelphia with Earl Bryant and Joel Stevenson, Drew pursued his legal and law enforcement career in Kentucky, developing his connections to the local police force. While Brad built a world involving the Chagra brothers, his cousin Larry and my father, Drew built a separate world with Bill Canan, Mike Kelly and Henry Vance.

The high school friends stayed in contact throughout their separate adult enterprises, Brad in the waste business and Drew on the first Lexington Narcotics Squad. As former military trained soldiers, they both worked for the CIA. The truth was much simpler than proposed by the sensationalized true crime television shows, podcasts and amateur sleuths.

What began as an honor code between two military academy friends seeking to do good with their extensive training, turned out to be a deadly and dangerous lifestyle. When Brad Bryant and Drew Thornton decided to use their training from the Army and Marine Corp to aid in a top secret mission to infiltrate the country's drug culture at the outset of America's War on Drugs, their fate was sealed. This was pre-Pablo Escobar. It was anyone's guess where it was all headed. There was no rule book. Marijuana trafficking in 1977 was the wild west.

Necessity being the mother of invention, Brad and Drew invented Executive Protection Services. It was an easy sell, as extremely capable military men, to present themselves as characters who could protect a high-profile customer from any danger they might encounter. Jamiel Alexander Chagra was a drug smuggler from El Paso who was reported to have been responsible for 85% of the marijuana circulating at the time. If you smoked pot in the late 1970s and early 80's, it probably came from Jimmy Chagra. Brad and Drew put out security offers to make the company appear legitimate but never took on any other clients. When opportunities came their way, they passed, staying focused on the task at hand, which was Chagra. Joseph Daniel Chandler was Vice President of Caesar's Palace and host to Lee Chagra and his brother, Jimmy. The two eccentric gamblers bet millions at the casino on a regular basis, making them my father's most valued customers.

"Did Daddy know you had a new security business?" I asked Uncle Brad.

"Yeah, he knew I had a personal security business," he said. "That's the way he introduced me to the Chagras. I told him we were open for business. He knew that part, so he was able to introduce me to the Chagras as a source of security for Lee and Jimmy."

It's hard for me to imagine Uncle Brad working as anyone's security. It didn't match his reality at the time as a businessman, the president of his own waste company with a mansion in Philadelphia. I asked if he had ever served as a source of protection for anyone else. The answer was no. He had never done personal security for another human being. The ploy was concocted by himself and Drew. It was not the idea of the CIA. It was something they structured to get on the inside. They were painstakingly closed-mouthed regarding their plans because in that realm, there was always an opportunity to be compromised. Brad never knew who he could trust. Any number of people could have turned on them, traded their information for other intelligence. Every move, including this new security detail, was kept close to the vest.

"Our mission was to develop connections to each thing, each issue, which was very involved, very complicated," said Uncle Brad as he attempted to explain the depth of secrecy surrounding this spy game. "We had to accomplish certain things before we could take the next level… the next step and gain confidence of certain people we were trying to get to know. We had to do certain things to make things happen. Obviously, we had to protect ourselves, protect our families and protect our associates and at the same time accomplish what we were trying to accomplish. This wasn't day one, day two, day three. This was basically… you have to take it very patiently, at the pace you could live with and accomplish without compromising anything else."

Learning about the planning process of a contracted operation is mind-boggling, exhausting and could turn anyone's sense of reality upside down. If there was a map of secret agents around the world, which I'm sure exists in one form or another, it would be horrifying to see how many men and women are presently in the process of cooking up their own self-destroying scenario. It would be staggering to see for one moment the thousands of individuals, from mansions to motels around the globe, breaking their heads over life-threatening schemes that might or might not move forward a mission contracted by the FBI, CIA, DEA or any unnamed agency purporting to do the 'right thing'.

When I asked my uncle what parts of the world he was dealing with, he rattled off the usual suspects in the world of drug and arms trading, "Guatemala, Mexico, Nicaragua, Venezuela…"

"How much time did you spend in those places?"

"As little as possible," he chuckled. "Yep. As little as possible."

"Did you have fake names wherever you went?"

"Oh, we had all kinds of fake names," Uncle Brad said. "Pocketsful of fake names, credentials and everything else."

I couldn't imagine what it would be like to be a spy, to carry a fake name and cast yourself in a variety of scenarios as someone you were not. My naiveté guided me to picture a man living in constant apprehension. I asked my uncle if he was always afraid.

"I was never scared of anything honey," Uncle Brad said in an upbeat tone. "Frankly, that was never a thought. You have to be cautious, and you had to be prepared but fear could not complicate your life. You had to be prepared and you had to be disciplined, period. There could never be a point where fear was ever a consideration."

I realize now, if you walked around in a state of perpetual unease, you would not make a very good spy. The truth is, it's no stretch to imagine Uncle Brad throwing himself into a dangerous environment. To say he has a cool, calm, demeanor is an understatement. In fact, he strikes me as someone who could walk into a cell with Hannibal Lector without flinching. Why he was like this intrigued me. How did he manage to split his time and his personality, heavily steeped in two very different worlds? What compelled my mother's brother to live in a world of peril is still a mystery, where at every turn his life could be taken from him in an instant.

"Brad was a guest at our house once," Fred Morelli, former Illinois judge and defense attorney remembered, "I had to go somewhere, and he was with my wife, Maria, for a couple hours. After he left, she said, 'he is the most polite, soft spoken, well-mannered person I've ever met. I talked to him for two hours and he didn't tell me anything.'"

With this extraordinary amount of restraint, the CIA kept Bradley Bryant working for fifteen years following that initial meeting at the motel outside Cincinnati with Drew. There was a steady stream of projects and missions, people to get to and get beyond. Brad somberly unwraps his thought process of the decade in question with a phrase he repeats again and again, "We were trying to accomplish something."

Brad had a handler based in Savannah who was always aware of his comings and goings. My mother says he talks about the man with warmth to this day. I wondered if he lost faith in who were the good guys and who were the bad ones. I believe he did, rapidly after willingly giving himself over to be 'handled'.

"You know honey," Uncle Brad said, "I pretty much focused on the people I was dealing with. I dealt with primarily one person, that way I could trust them and that was it. I didn't trust many people. You had to be prepared for it. I made a commitment and had to fulfill my commitments. You know you think you're... you want to think you're good people, think you are."

Douglas Valentine speaks to this issue, "It destroys people and their families who have to live with the people who are under this cloud... under this gag order." Valentine has seen countless families shattered when someone they love has lived under the thumb of national security organizations. Knowing that to speak about any number of things could endanger you and your family would make anyone paranoid, neurotic and repressed. This mode of operation is made infinitely worse when the worker bee is disavowed and discarded.

The strain was too much for Brad's marriage and it dissolved in a very unhappy way. My aunt was the most beautiful woman I had ever seen, with long, silky, streaked hair. She wore knee high boots and colorful scarves around her head. She was also smart as a whip with a great sense of humor. They were so much in love and had three adorable children. I know the shattering of his family was Brad's biggest heartbreak and regret of his life.

"It broke up pretty much when I went to Savannah," Uncle Brad admitted. "I tried to hold things together, but I couldn't. I was gone constantly, back and forth, back and forth. We tried to hold it together, but it just didn't work. Of course, I couldn't talk to her about anything. It destroyed my life, honey," Uncle Brad said finally. "Our lives were in complete darkness. Everything we did. Our lies were our lives. Your lies are your life."

PART II

A PIRATE LOOKS AT FORTY

Erin Chandler

CHAPTER
TEN

"I do my own killing..."
—Benny Binion

Long before Las Vegas morphed into the Disneyland we see today, money, glamour and murder kept it contained and exclusive. It was still in the clutches of mob bosses when Joseph Daniel Chandler, came onto the scene. Daddy moved there in 1973, over a decade before large corporations bought up the property so flip-flopped masses could swarm in like locusts. Nowadays, you couldn't find the old Las Vegas with an archeologists trowel. Nothing resembles the place where from a barren desert, a single bedazzled strip emerged. You could see the whole thing from one end to the other and there was a good deal of space between every hotel and casino, each with its own individual character. Today it all blends together like one big ride. I have no desire to go back to the place my father lived from 1973-2004, the place I spent every summer and holiday from 1973 until the nineties. I get anxiety just thinking about the besieged fortress, overgrown with drunken frat boys and families in shorts and sandals slurping up frozen sugar. The same Nevada real estate I witnessed so stylishly hosting Sammy Davis Jr., Frank Sinatra and Ann Margaret is now covered with moving sidewalks and monorails connecting theme parks carelessly doused in tinsel. The new Las Vegas has less to do with the old one than it does Pigeon Forge or Fort Lauderdale.

Only those of us fortunate enough to have witnessed the exclusive, gaudy opulence of that bravely hedonistic world pulsating in the middle of the Mojave Desert know how different it was back then. In the seventies, it seemed Chan and I were the only kids in Caesar's Palace. You would be hard pressed to find another pre-teen in the casino save for the Osmond Brothers or the occasional child of an entertainer or professional gambler. It was a different crowd, a dressed-up crowd, a more dangerous crowd. Cars blew up, and people 'disappeared.' Not everyone working in the casino could safely assume he would make it through the day if he angered the wrong person. Daddy's close friend and associate, Ash Resnick, our frequent coffee shop lunch date, had his car blown up in the Caesar's Palace parking lot. Ash narrowly escaped assassination, but it did little to dissuade his high profile around the casino. Another Caesar's executive was not so lucky when his car exploded in broad daylight at the rear of the hotel.

My father was well aware of the danger, "That's a guy you don't even want to be on his good side." He told Chan and me about the little Italian man approaching our table with hooded eyes and a three-piece suit. After numerous handshakes and back pats, I realized we were obviously on his good side. It was an education I am still processing. My father raised us in an environment that was equal parts moral high ground and seedy criminality. Between high society, Kentucky horse country and high crime Las Vegas, there was a lot to absorb. Not least of which was the fatal influence of those two Lebanese brothers from El Paso.

Lee and Jimmy Chagra were the biggest players in town which made the criminal defense attorney and his smuggling sibling Daddy's top priority. I pull a familiar scene from my memory which took place during that perpetual night of Caesar's Palace. No matter what time of day, neon slot machines flashed, and it was always time for a half-naked woman in a Roman costume to bring you a free drink and a dealer in a white button-down shirt and black slacks to deal you into the game. I remember Lee and Jimmy standing on the periphery of the Blackjack tables, my father with one ear in their conversation, the other attending to someone else. I remember Uncle Brad, standing next to them on that gaudy red and gold carpet, stiff, serious, stone faced. I wonder about that fated conversation when the gambler revealed to the casino host's brother-in-law that he was not only a high roller but also a drug smuggler of the highest order.

Gene Ganucheau was there from the beginning of Daddy, Uncle Brad and the Chagra's tenure in Vegas. As a casino pit boss and Blackjack dealer, Gene was ensconced in our life in the desert. He was part of the family. The football player from Biloxi, Mississippi had transferred to the University of Kentucky before making his way out to Las Vegas. The young quarterback who majored in recreation administration was friends with my grandfather, Happy Chandler. A former football coach himself, Pappy was in the habit of attending University of Kentucky football practice every day.

"I read in the paper where Dan, your dad, had gone to Vegas as a casino host," Gene told me. "I called Happy, and I said, Happy can you introduce me to your son?"

Pappy made the introduction. Gene took it and ran. He had his college diploma sent to Daddy's condo behind the Hilton, at 744 Tam O' Shanter. From the moment Gene arrived out west in 1974, he and Dan Chandler got on famously. They were both carefree southern boys and athletes at a party that was just getting started.

Gene is now an incredibly young, seventy-year-old man back home in Mississippi, happily twenty-two years sober. He runs casinos himself now and attributes this to the knowledge and experience he gained in Las Vegas with Dan Chandler. "Your dad opened so many doors for me it's unbelievable. And not so much opening doors, but he just knew everybody. The first week I was there, we went to the Alan King tennis tournament at Caesar's. Here I am country kid from Biloxi, Mississippi, I looked in front of me, the seat in front of me was Johnny Carson, okay? So here I am... is that guy Johnny Carson? Before I knew it, we were talking to him and then we went into the celebrity tent. Buddy Hackett comes up and starts telling jokes right there. So many people... Willie Nelson, we went backstage with Willie Nelson so many times and up in rooms. I mean, Andy Williams... you saw them all too, you probably saw a lot more than I did. I'm telling you, it was unbelievable. Your dad could talk to anybody from the President of the United States to the biggest drug dealers in the world."

He certainly could and it taught my brother and me an invaluable lesson to see our father treat valet parkers and phone operators with as much enthusiasm and respect, using the same eye contact and humor, as he did his boss or some internationally famous movie star. He loved people and like his daughter after him, he loved life. Chan took after our mother in matters of sentimentality. I took after Daddy, inheriting his eternal optimism and appreciation of the moment. During those first years in Nevada, those formative years as children, we drove our black Bronco every few days out to the desert mountains surrounding Vegas. It seemed of utmost importance to our father that he impress upon Chan and me the life lessons he had gathered thus far. He was forever preaching and more often than not, those sermons came in the form of song lyrics by Glen Frye, Jimmy Buffet, Jerry Reed or John Denver. Those blazing days, sitting on various cliffs of the Red Rock Canyon, there was always a six pack of Coors and Kentucky Fried Chicken on a blanket. The basic message he so desperately tried to get into our small heads was to enjoy life. Enjoy life and love our mother, even though she made the terrible mistake of splitting our family up. The other vital lesson was don't trust anyone. The only people we could trust were right there on the mountain, Chan, Daddy and me… and Mamma. Then again and again, always again, was enjoy life. My take-away was a powerful feeling of strength, togetherness, breathing in the mountain air, taking in the open road and a painfully romantic vision of living on the edge of society. Someone was always on the

8-track singing about the border, a man was either running from the law or soaking up the sun in a sailboat heading the opposite direction of normal.

"I know, I know," Gene Ganucheau nods as I recount these memories.

"What was that?" I ask.

"I don't know. I never knew. I never met Dan until I went to Vegas. I did know Happy, I knew he was twice governor, you know, Commissioner of Baseball but I didn't know if something in Dan's background was making him think like a criminal, or something," he laughed. "I didn't know. I also heard that Happy was going to run for president and they wouldn't let him because he was too honest, did you ever hear that?"

I had and it didn't surprise me. My grandfather, Albert Benjamin Chandler, was honest as the day is long, filled with integrity, a pillar of strength, and sobriety. Although my grandfather was not as nice as my father by a long shot, not as empathetic or as charming. Pappy was not warm and kind with his family like he was with his public. My cousins and I laugh as we imitate him, screaming, "GOOOooooooddamn it! Close the GOoooddamn window!" Yes, he gave big bone crushing hugs but he didn't like being questioned, didn't like being anything but the boss. This is typical, I gather, for men who have accomplished so much worldwide. Pappy also didn't like the fact that my mother left my father. He made a power move that would change all of our lives irreparably. When Mamma began dating a professor at the University of Kentucky, Paul August Knipping, he used his considerable influence to have him fired. The man who would be my stepfather was already in his fifties, twenty years older than Lynne Bryant Chandler, and a popular health and biology professor with tenure at the university. He was let go without explanation. This prompted Paul's swift acceptance to a college in Farmington, Maine, setting in motion a quickie marriage with my mother and the removal of Chan and me from our last remnants of security. From 1975, we never again had a permanent residence in our old Kentucky home. We visited our grandparents and cousins, but life began then and there, at ten and twelve, a chaotic shuffle between Las Vegas and Maine, then Las Vegas and Lubbock, Texas, where Paul took a position teaching at Texas Tech for the rest of our school years.

Happy Chandler claimed his revenge on the man who hurt his baby boy even though it was to the detriment of his grandchildren. Pappy, in his Corydon, Kentucky accent, used to proclaim in disgust about our stepfather, "He has two livin' wives!" Paul was divorced and his ex-wife was indeed alive. As far as my mother dealing with my unruly, impossible to live with father, Pappy didn't have sympathy for any woman's unhappy plight. This was probably because his own mother abandoned the family when he was two years old. Whatever the case, Pappy spent his life unapologetically sitting in the front seat. Women and children in the back.

No matter, Dan Chandler idolized his father, spending his life touting Pappy as the greatest politician alive and believing everything he had was due to his father. Thankfully, Daddy took his emotional cues from his mother, Mildred Watkins Chandler. He was extraordinarily warm and generous just like Mammy. He also had a healthy sense of humor about himself where my grandfather absolutely did not.

I remember those first few summers living with Daddy after the divorce. We didn't have any money, but we had dinner every night at the most expensive steak houses on the strip. As a casino executive, my father had the 'power of the pen' so we just signed for expensive dinners even if we couldn't afford a proper tip. Daddy kept a big jar in our little kitchen filled with silver dollars, so we loaded up before we went out and always left a big stack of silver dollars for the waiter. Everything in those days had pirate-like energy, everyone was getting away with something.

"Your dad, if it wasn't for him, I would have starved to death," Gene remembered. "We went into the coffee shop, I had breakfast, steak and eggs, just about every morning with him. I was poor as could be, I didn't have any money. He didn't have any money either at that time, but we're riding around like we're millionaires."

Speaking of modern-day pirates, Gene met Lee Chagra upon arrival. "It was at Caesar's Palace," he said. "I was always hanging out there and he was your dad's player, big, huge player. Probably the biggest player in town. He was the best. Oh, he was great. Jimmy was too. Both of them just had hearts of gold. Of course, they both had a ton of money. I had heard rumors about Jimmy, and I knew Lee was a great attorney because he used to get all the drug dealers out of trouble. We got on Caesar's plane, we took this group from El Paso to a baseball game in St. Louis, that's when I first met him. That was near the time Jimmy was really rolling."

At twenty-three years old, Ganucheau was an innocent bystander with a front row seat as Daddy and Uncle Brad played with fire. While Brad was gathering information for the CIA to take the Chagras down, my father was gathering resources to build them up, doing everything in his power to encourage the Chagras to lead their high-flying life at Caesar's Palace. He signed off millions of dollars in casino cash credit, provided presidential suites, private jets, and limos at their service. Shielded by the glitz and glamour of the gambling establishment, a 'When in Rome' attitude gave them all license to be as decadent as the job required.

Chan and I were under the same small roof, but our eyes were focused on what appealed to each of us individually. Mine were on the showgirls and boutiques, Andy Williams back up dancers and The Lennon Sisters glittery costumes, rehearsals, fake tap tracks, beaded clothes, and feather boas. Chan was into his pool boy job at Caesar's, carrying towels, setting up lounge chairs and hanging out at the tennis pavilion with pros, Jimmy Conners, Chris Evert and Pancho Gonzales. Our entertainment and sports heroes became actual daily companions, so the dark underbelly of our shaky foundation went completely over our heads… for the time being.

"Yeah, ya'll were spoiled brats," Gene laughed. "Just kidding. I tell you what, your dad though, he did spoil ya'll, 'cause he would do anything… and I know it probably had a lot to do with coming from a split family and stuff but anything you guys wanted he gave ya'll. You know he was so good to Chan and you when you went to California. Chan was a little hard to handle sometimes. You knew that."

It would have been an act of God had he not been. My brother and I grew up smack dab in the middle of more illegality, more straight-up gangster business than imaginable. Truth be told, there were shadier characters than the Chagras around town, a different crop of outlaw far more ferocious. I shudder to think of the countless hired killers we passed sitting at Cleopatra's Barge, prostitutes on their arms, smiling and toasting. The lifestyle was more than a flirtation with amorality, it was the lion's den.

Bluegrass Sons

Dan and Erin Chandler with friends, Miami Jockey club owner, Walter Troutman and Lexington's George Carey at Benny Binion's Horseshoe

CHAPTER
ELEVEN

Blood Aces

Benny Binion was another nefarious character who made his way out to the desert town. My father was enchanted with the image of Benny arriving in Las Vegas just after World War II with two million dollars cash in suitcases and his extended family packed in a Cadillac. What he didn't perhaps know or at least care to acknowledge, was that Binion was one of the most dangerous criminals Texas had ever seen. According to the book *Blood Aces: The Wild Ride of Benny Binion, the Texas Gangster Who Created Vegas Poker* by Doug Swanson, Binion was a ruthless gangster with henchmen at the ready. "I do my own killin'," the old cowboy famously repeated even in his later years.

Chan and I spent countless days lunching with the robust old outlaw in a bolo tie and cowboy hat at his casino coffee shop. The owner of Binion's Horseshoe was clearly fond of our father because we had carte blanche at his casino. Maybe it was Daddy's cleverness and gusto or just his pedigree that made Dan Chandler seem like such a good candidate for mayor of Las Vegas, but Binion offered to bankroll the effort. My father respectfully passed. I think a failed 1960s run for Congress in Kentucky was all the politics he had in him.

The mutual admiration continued and when in need of a safe haven one hot summer night, it was to Benny's bosom we were delivered. Chan and I were shaken from a dead sleep when we were living in the Carriage House across the street from the Aladdin Hotel. The apartment was high up in the last room of an empty floor at the far end of the strip. Dan Chandler hustled his eight and ten-year-olds out of their beds and into a waiting cab. God only knows what threat came to prompt Daddy to rush us out in our pajamas at 3:00 am, but we were hurried downtown for safety. Binion's Horseshoe was on the dirtier, seedier side of Vegas, far from the main drag. Chan and I sat on the gold paisley carpeted stairs, peering through the banister out over the stale casino. Our father was below in a sea of Blackjack tables, talking to good ol' Benny. Daddy looked up and smiled, raising his fist in the air, indicating mission accomplished. Through the old wooden railing, we raised our tiny fists back in unison.

My memory of smiling demurely, looking on as the old cowboy patted my father on the back makes me sad for the little girl in the clinging, clanging, neon casino in the middle of the night. More sympathy comes for my ten-year-old brother, trying to grow up with an out-of-control father. A few years later, when he began to act out as a young teen, Chan was sent to Binion's dude ranch in Wyoming to 'straighten out'. Daddy considering Benny Binion our savior is a level of bad judgement hard to reconcile. Maybe Chan got some much-needed fresh air and a few horse riding skills, but I doubt the cowboys running the ranch had a moral compass to which any young man should aspire.

Former Las Vegas mayor and mob lawyer, Oscar Goodman, naturally feels differently about Benny Binion. I first met Oscar on the set of the *Bionic Woman* with Lindsay Wagner. I was eleven years old in 1976 and it was my first encounter with movie making magic. Daddy convinced them to let me ride in the back seat of a car loaded with cameras on its hood. Oscar was filming a cameo and sat in the front seat with Lindsay. We drove down the strip as they played out the scene and exchanged dialogue. I remained off camera, hunkered down in the backseat absolutely thrilled to pieces. It was another small step toward my inevitable foray into show business. Oscar spoke to me on record in 2022. I knew he would not take kindly to me speaking harshly of our old friend Benny Binion at this stage of the game.

"He was a pretty tough dude," was as far as I ventured.

"Well, he was a tough dude," Oscar allowed politely in his long-surviving Philadelphia accent. "But a very... I think very gentlemanly towards ladies."

This lawyerly statement was offered up to settle my feminine ideals as well as my delicate eyes and ears. "He was certainly sweet to us," I softly matched his polite demeanor as we discussed the cold-blooded killer. After all, it was no lie,

Mr. Binion was nice to me. He might have even murdered for us had we asked. As a little girl and later a teenager, it was impressed upon me that if anyone was cruel or mistreated me, it was within my power to make a phone call, and someone would set them straight. I knew that meant threatened, beaten up or even killed. Instead of horrifying me as it does now, I felt powerful, untouchable. It was comforting to feel taken care of.

"I can't see him being any way other than that," said Oscar, trained to defend and block out the most heinous of crimes.

I wasn't going to quibble with Mr. Goodman, who had represented Uncle Brad, my father, my brother, as well as Lee and Jimmy Chagra. Oscar was a fixture in Daddy's Vegas world as much as Benny Binion, woven into the fabric of Nevada. That tight inner circle protected their own. If it wasn't your thing to shoot people on the street for stealing a few hundred dollars but your buddy's son did just that, it was perfectly acceptable to look the other way and enjoy a club sandwich at his casino coffee shop. Suspend your belief, pretend everyone's all good with the Lord.

"There was a time I had lunch with him every single day at a table that he had reserved for himself at the Horseshoe," Goodman said jocularly, recalling Benny's wiles. "I always get a kick out of it because Harry Claiborne, I don't know if you ever met Judge Claiborne, but he was a friend of your dad, I'm sure. Everyone was a friend of your dad, and your dad was a friend of everybody. It would be a natural. Eddy LaRue, who was a private investigator, he used to eat with us. Teddy Binion (Benny's son) would come by. I liked Teddy very, very much. We would always eat the same thing. I was always on a diet in those days so I would always have lettuce and tomato with a little vinegar and olive oil. Claiborne would have ham hocks and lima beans and Benny Binion used to eat squirrel stew, head and all!"

"I bet that's the same table where we had lunch a thousand times," I laughed along, suspending my own sense of morality.

"Okay then," Oscar laughed heartily. "You'll remember that little squirrel head always popped up with its glassy eyes and buck teeth. For a guy like me to imagine anybody eating squirrel…"

There was one law abiding character in our Vegas world, Richard P. Crane. Originally from Connecticut, my father's best friend and lawyer relocated to California early in his career. Dick Crane was the president of the Bel Air Country Club in Los Angeles. He was also the former head of the Organized Crime and Racketeering Strike Force for the U.S. Department of Justice in the thirteen western states. Dick Crane wasn't a creature of Las Vegas, and he was a touch stone for my rambunctious father. He is one person I can talk to who recognizes, among other things, our dangerously close friendship with Benny Binion.

"Yeah, he was tough," Dick remembered quietly of the Texas gangster. "He was tough. We investigated him up one side and down the other."

Dick was only twenty-nine years old when he was named Attorney in Charge, the youngest in the nation with the title. He ran the entire strike force with a team of guys throughout the west, investigating and prosecuting the Mafia. "I personally took on the task to get them out of Nevada, which during the time in the 60s and 70s, Nevada was all mobbed up. That was my job, to bring these guys down. And we did… we got rid of every damn one of 'em, but it took us a while."

I wondered what Dick Crane thought about the new breed of arguably rougher outlaws that cropped up in Vegas when the mob was run out. We discussed the book, *Blood Aces* and how the author claims back in Texas, Benny Binion had adversaries murdered and occasionally buried alive.

"Yeah, he was vicious," Dick said casually.

"And Daddy sent Chan to Binion's ranch in Wyoming when he was a teenager?" I nearly pleaded. "Like it was some respected children's camp?"

"Mmm hmmm… yeah," Dick had no answer.

"That wasn't very smart," I stated the obvious.

"Well, your dad did some things that in retrospect," he laughed, "were regrettable. But I loved him unequivocally."

Dick and his beautiful wife Janie provided a stable escape from the madness more times than I can possibly count. Dick and Janie's home at the end of a cul-de-sac in their gated community a block from the sea was the opposite of escaping to Binion's Horseshoe. My father lived with the Cranes in the Pacific Palisades for months at a time over their decades long friendship. Daddy sprawled out in every room, wandering around in his boxers like he owned the place. Throughout my twenties and thirties, that was the place I met up with my father when he was in my adopted home of Los Angeles. In contrast, I felt like a rug rat in their bright and spotless home, keeping my purses and duffel bags close so not to take up too much space.

"Lookin' good, Hollywood!" Daddy would say as we lounged by Dick and Janie's pool, a few feet from their tennis courts. This was the world we aspired to once we were able to climb out of Vegas.

Bluegrass Sons

Joseph Daniel Chandler with Lee Chagra and his family at Caesar's Palace
Circus Maximus Showroom, circa 1974

CHAPTER
TWELVE

Dirty Dealing

Lee and Jimmy Chagra's great grandparents were born in Lebanon. Their grandparents migrated to Mexico and eventually settled in El Paso where the brothers were born and raised. El Paso is a military town, a family-oriented place despite the fact it's only a short, rocky walk through the desert from Juarez, one of the most dangerous cities in Mexico. "Everyone was smuggling something," Jimmy Chagra said of the border town, "whether it was gold or silver or carpets." He must have had good business sense because it is no small feat for a carpet salesman to go from trading gold, silver, and rugs to being one of the biggest drug traffickers in America. By most accounts, Jimmy is the black sheep of the Chagra clan. He's crude with a penchant for strip clubs and prostitutes. He introduced his nephew, Leader and Leader's best friend, my brother Chan, to their first when they were barely fifteen years old.

Leader's father, Lee and his brother Jimmy, were as Oscar Goodman, lawyer and friend of both men recounted, one hundred percent a different kind of people in every way shape and form. "You know Lee was very educated, number one in his law school class in Texas," Oscar Goodman exhaled over the phone wires. "He was a gentleman. Lee was charismatic. Every time I saw him, he was wearing a white suit with the white boots, and he had his walking stick with, I think it was a silver handle if I'm not mistaken. Big cowboy hat. Very handsome, very articulate, very smart… and Jimmy was a hustler."

While Jimmy was the one that got things done, so to speak, Lee was the clean-cut businessman, the brains, and the one who developed a close friendship with my father. It was clear to my young eyes that Lee Chagra was magnetic. Women from all walks of life flocked to the side of the snazzy, gentle man.

"He made me feel like the Queen of the Nile," Ann Hollingsworth told the story of sitting on Lee's lap on the way to Anita Madden's Pre-Derby bash forty years ago. My mother's lovely and sheltered best friend worked in the registrar's office at Sayre school in Lexington and was the parent of two small children attending there. "I had never been around a man at that point in my life who was so charming and so gracious... so sensitive to a woman's desires that she doesn't even know she has," Ann blushed.

It was the first Friday of May 1974. Daddy and his girlfriend Delores had flown in Caesar's private jet from Las Vegas to Kentucky for the Derby with their friend Lee Chagra. It was certainly what Dan Chandler was paid to do, ingratiate himself to professional gamblers who frequented Caesar's, but in the case of Lee, it became personal. Daddy really liked Lee and Lee really liked my father. It would be hard to dislike either man, but those two vibrant personalities in their prime, together in that place at that time, were a sight to behold. When Ann stopped by Uncle Ben and Aunt Toss's (Daddy's older brother and his wife), she had not planned on going to Anita Madden's bacchanalian extravaganza.

"Dan and Delores were there. Delores was pregnant, largely pregnant, and Lee was there," Ann remembered. "Dan says, 'come on, let's go, let's go!' like he always does, without any planning. Toss took me up and put some of her clothes on me and we headed to the Madden party. All of us got in the same car. Ben and Toss and Lee and I were in the backseat, if you can imagine. Fortunately, we were all small people but when I got ready to get in the car there was no place except Lee's lap! So, Lee says, 'come on, come on, we can make it! We can make it!' and it was this big folderol of Dan's, you know, getting things done. I'm just in shock because I've never done anything like this before. Everybody was just laughing, and it was just one big kind of laughing thing. I was very, very shy, because I was not... as strange as it sounds... I was not experienced. I was just confused and shy and sort of prim and proper at that stage."

When they arrived at the party, Ann was amazed at the spectacle. Women in scantily clad outfits spilled out of an enormous tent. Men in loin cloths carried silver trays of cocktails. It was like Studio 54 in the middle of a Kentucky horse farm. During the course of the evening Lee Chagra asked Ann to dance. Lee was small, and not necessarily attractive in any way Ann had previously registered attraction. He didn't look like anyone she had ever noticed before. They danced. "You are so lovely," Lee said before gently inquiring, "tell me about yourself."

"What do you mean?" Ann asked him.

"You don't know who you are, do you?" Chagra smiled, cupping the small of her back. "You are just gorgeous."

The dark, mysterious stranger with a magic touch made her feel like there was nobody at that party who had what she had. Ann remembered breathlessly, "he told me he had children, that he adored his children. Just adored his children. But that's all. He didn't talk about business. He didn't talk about money. He didn't say anything that would inflate his own image or ego. It was like he was so secure within himself he didn't need to. I didn't know who he was from Adam's off ox!"

With the confidence of a doctor of philosophy and the expertise of a clinical psychiatrist, Lee Chagra analyzed Ann's dissolved marriage. Her first husband simply didn't know what to do with her, Lee explained, didn't understand her power. She was transfixed. On their way home, she again sat on his lap. There was no forwardness or sexual suggestion. Instead, he caressed her and held her like a baby. "I know how this feels to you," Lee said softly, "I know how awkward this feels to you." This produced a feeling Ann had yet to experience in this lifetime. It was the feeling of someone knowing you better than you knew yourself.

"After that... after the evening went on, I just was... I just was in love with him!" Ann and I laughed until we cried. We both understood the naiveté infused in that scene, easy to conjure as yesterday. Ann Hollingsworth never saw or heard from Lee Chagra again.

The scene my mother's lifelong friend recalls made me realize that Lee's charm and magnetism was inherited by Lee's son, Leader and in turn, my brother. Chan and Leader were inseparable from the time they were fourteen, if not in the same state, they were on the phone plotting their next move. Chan and Leader mirrored each other, effortlessly developing the kind of hypnotizing allure with the ladies Lee had. Chan didn't get this swagger from our father. Daddy was not a ladies' man. Dan Chandler was loud and boisterous and funny. That sexuality mixed with what I would refer to as a submissive nature with women was most likely gained witnessing the smooth character of Lee Chagra. Chan and Leader carried themselves with a seamless mixture of humble, non-threatening passivity and arrogance. Like Lee, they wore matching bracelets that spelled out FREEDOM. The two developed a soft, almost feminine touch when addressing women and a respectful, confident one with men, and when needed, they were fearless and bold with fast swinging fists.

Lucy Backer Cox recalls hanging out with Chan and Leader in Lexington when they were all in their early twenties and she was in law school at the University of Kentucky. She remembers the two young men mesmerizing a gaggle of attractive young law students. They couldn't get enough. "These are the smartest girls that only date preppy guys," Lucy laughs. "Chan and Leader come in and they've got guns and they've got drugs and sports cars and there's some shit going on like a judge that was murdered."

Chan Chandler, Leader and Dina Chagra, Lexington, Kentucky

Chan and Leader came by it honestly. Their role models were Brad Bryant, Dan Chandler and Lee Chagra, how could they not operate from inside of the velvet rope? When you are forming an opinion of the world at large from a unique perspective of male figures operating outside of societal norms, you're going to stand out. This was a world like no other and it was their father's world, so by extension, it was theirs.

"I think your father liked the Chagras," said Dick Crane. "And I think your father got too close to them. At one time, he asked me to represent them... this was after I'd left the government... asked if I wanted to represent them legally and I said 'no way'. That's an Oscar Goodman representation, not me."

Dick Crane continued to warn Dan Chandler about the danger inherent in his relationship with the Chagras. "I told your dad on more than one occasion," he said, "you've gotten too close to these guys, get away from them. But he wouldn't listen to me, you know that. He'd listen to me, but he wouldn't follow through. Not if it... not if it... your father was a hedonist," Dick laughed. "And I loved him more than anybody, any man in my life, but he did some stupid things."

Speaking of stupid things, my father allowed Jimmy Chagra to hide one million dollars in the walls of our home in the Las Vegas Country Club at 744 Tam O'Shanter. Unfortunately, it's no stretch for me to imagine someone hammering through the walls of the small two-bedroom condo, stuffing wads of cash behind the thin plaster where I spent day after day, week after week, month after month, often completely alone, for a decade. I'm sure Jimmy gave Daddy $20,000.00 or so for this service, chump change for Chagra.

"I believe the part about your dad storing money at his house for the Chagras," Dick said. "I can see Dan doing that. As stupid as that is, I can see him doing that."

"Well, he absolutely did..." I shake my head.

"I know," Dick agreed. "He was a loyal guy and the Chagras were making his career because they were the biggest players in the history of legalized gaming in Nevada and they were your Daddy's customers. Dan was a god at Caesar's at the time because he had these guys losing millions at Caesar's so your dad was walking on water. He wanted to protect that so I can see him doing something stupid like hiding money for the Chagras. I can see that. I can tell you this, I don't think he ever knew the extent of their drug dealing."

Chan Chandler with his Uncle Brad Bryant

CHAPTER
THIRTEEN

The Real Narcos

It's hard to imagine Bradley Bryant was not worried about his brother-in-law, who he loved dearly. For him to assume Dan Chandler would be left categorically unscathed, out of danger physically and legally, seems naïve in the extreme. I asked my uncle if he thought it was dangerous for Daddy to be so closely interwoven with the Chagras in the middle of a covert CIA investigation.

"He did his casino host thing. I did not think it was a problem," Uncle Brad stated adamantly. It is his opinion that my father was never in jeopardy during this perilous spy game. "I did not try to walk him outside of that scope," he reiterated. "Very carefully structured him. He was within the frame of what he was involved with and that was it. He did not… I never asked him… never had a conversation with him outside of that range. He didn't know I was trying to meet the Chagras. He didn't even know it. I just did it because of his situation. I knew what was going on. When I flew out there and of course stayed at Caesars, I knew they were there so I just… we just made it happen."

I hated to think of Daddy as a pawn, outwitted by his young brother-in-law. Strange to think Uncle Brad had the power to "structure him" in any way. I'm certain my father never imagined such a dynamic had taken root. It brought forth unnerving images in my imagination of Brad holding Daddy's shoulders, physically adjusting him on that treacherous battlefield made of ornate restaurants, green felt Blackjack tables, and oak wood chip trays. It brought back sense memories of countless days standing in a cold, dark casino sports book, looking up at the neon spread sheet as my father placed the day's bet, the sun high and arrogant, scorching everything outside.

There is no doubt in my mind Daddy knew the Chagras were conducting themselves in a matter not completely sympatico with the authorities, but I am just as certain he didn't intend to be a conduit to a government sponsored infiltration. He never would have knowingly delivered a spy into their heavily vaulted, seemingly impenetrable penthouse suite.

Jimmy Chagra had no clue Dan Chandler's brother-in-law, Brad Bryant, was anything other than a source of security. He was never suspicious. Uncle Brad never introduced any opportunity for Jimmy to think he was anything other than the main man. Jimmy's ego was such that he was blinded by the attention and protection from his new military trained 'security.' To assure his safety, he wanted Brad to go everywhere with him. It turns out, the job was usually accompanying him to strip clubs.

"Trash, road trash," Uncle Brad says now. "I mean he really was trash. Jimmy would... frankly, Jimmy at night... he wanted to go out to strip clubs and things like that. That was pretty much it. He was never anything other than the casinos."

Uncle Brad took it one step at a time, with extreme patience and methodology. He and his associates made sure they were there for Jimmy, day or night, anytime he needed anything. Eventually, he gained Chagra's supreme trust. He convinced this veritable stranger that he was not only capable of flying an airplane to South America and picking up hundreds of pounds of marijuana and delivering it safely back to the United States but that he would not squeal if he was caught. Allowing his security detail to be part of his smuggling operation, Jimmy was in a very vulnerable position. Carelessly, he unleashed significant drug connections all over the world.

There was never a rush to get to this bird's eye view of Jimmy Chagra's smuggling operation. Uncle Brad was never in a hurry to introduce himself into that part of Jimmy's life. Eventually, Jimmy began to talk to him about opportunities to make more money. That is how the conversation started that eventually brought Brad Bryant into the Chagra's inner circle.

Like Jimmy Lambert before him, Chagra was a resource for the CIA. Again, my uncle phrased it like this, "Jimmy

Chagra was a vehicle. Jimmy was simply a vehicle. He was a resource to get to the next level."

Jimmy Chagra unknowingly funded the investigation on himself. "Of course, the money had to come from him to finance the opportunity," Brad explained. "So, he advanced the money to buy an airplane. At the same time, we evolved into securing material for him and by doing that we had to make connections to where the stuff went, find out where the stuff went."

"Was Drew part of that deal?" I assumed.

"He knew about it. Was he a part of it? Some stuff he was a part of some stuff he wasn't. Different paths. But we knew what the other was doing. No, he wasn't involved with everything. You had to get through that relationship with those individuals to the next level, someone was controlling them so that's what we did. Drew never communicated with Chagra personally. I communicated."

"Did you find the pilot to do that? Did you find the crew to do that?"

"Drew found the crew," he said. "Drew found the crew in order to be involved with that. We tried to keep everything as distant as possible to protect each other so certain components... he provided financing for that and the connections."

The first plane flew to Colombia. Jimmy Chagra didn't know when it was taking off, where to or when. Once he gave up the connections, Brad communicated directly with those people about where they were going, what they were going to do and where the delivery point would be. Brad did not keep the CIA abreast of each step. He just let them know it was going to happen but didn't tell them when or where.

"No… hell no," Uncle Brad said when I asked if his 'handlers' knew every move. "Like I said, you never know who you could trust, kid. You assume but you never know."

The first delivery was flown into Lexington, Kentucky. It was a couple of thousand pounds. They set up the specifics, delivered it and Chagra's people picked it up simultaneously. They all got paid and it was on to the next step. The next step of course was another pickup and another delivery. They were in business. Completing several of these trips back and forth from Colombia, Brad usually dealt with the same people. Only occasionally was it someone new.

Infused with my Netflix and YouTube-fed imagination, my *Ozark* and *Narcos* drug cartel sensibilities, I thought of the infamous Escobar clan. Maybe Uncle Brad was dealing with the rival cartels that took down Escobar. I assumed it was one of the famous groups we now call by name but back in 1976, drug cartels didn't have the supermodel status they have now. My uncle schooled me when I asked what they were called. "They weren't called anything as far as I knew," Brad said abruptly. "We didn't even consider that. They were just people."

"They were just farmers growing marijuana?" I questioned.

"Right. Cocaine and marijuana, that was the major deal. And we just had to…" he shook his head before letting out a dark, resolved chuckle, "I mean it was ridiculous."

I pressed for an image, a picture of what the men looked like. Apparently, to Brad they were just normal people. My imagining it was anything else embarrassed me immediately. Here were local folks doing what needed to be done to satisfy whatever boss they worked under. Meeting the slick American who flew into town to buy what they were selling was part of a day's work. Their relationship was basic. He communicated with them like he would anyone else. There was no suspicion that Brad and his pilots were anything other than people who wanted to procure the drugs, pay the Colombians, and get paid themselves.

"Of course, they had security," Brad allowed. Security to me meant machine guns in the hands of men, boys, maybe women protecting their product. A firing squad came to mind. I pictured dead bodies lining the dusty streets of Juarez like I had seen in documentaries and wondered if the backwoods jungle where these exchanges took place was similar. I thought these 'normal people' were killing rampantly like in the movies. Surely my uncle witnessed machine guns go off, had to duck for cover, shimmy across the dirt and dive into a mud shack nearby. I imagined Brad witnessed people shot in the head by a Mexican drug lord on his shiny tile driveway in front of a mansion. The kingpin of my daydream would step over the slumped body and offer everyone a slab of beef.

I asked Uncle Brad if he could confirm my idea. Had he ever seen the farmers, the drug dealers or the drug lords kill anybody? "No, I never saw them kill anybody... them," he emphasized clearly. "I never saw them kill anybody."

I quietly put forth the question most prevalent in my mind. Had ever seen the CIA kill anyone? "Of course," he was so matter of fact it was chilling.

"And they justify it..." I asked softly, "how?"

"That's a good question," Uncle Brad chuckled darkly, "yeah, yeah."

Bluegrass Sons

Dan Chandler and long-time girlfriend, Delores

CHAPTER
FOURTEEN

Lawyers, Guns and Money

The private jet zoomed through the air with Daddy and Delores giggling like naughty teenagers. They were on their way to Guatemala with Uncle Brad. Delores was around thirty at the time, a gorgeous tomboy with a platinum pixie cut, small hips and giant boobs. Outfitted in a white silk shirt tucked into skintight blue jeans, she had a knife stuck down in her cowboy boots. This quintessential rhinestone cowgirl was tailor-made for Dan Chandler, the best of friends and lovers, fearlessly mixing amongst gods and monsters on their own personal circus ride. My father's long-time love even rode a bull in a rodeo one afternoon. She got on and hung on for longer than most cowboys. What was extraordinary is that it wasn't extraordinary for Delores, just another daredevil move, another adventure.

When I think of Daddy and Delores flying to Guatemala with Uncle Brad, I wonder how much they knew. Did they know Brad was hatching a plan for further drug transportation? Did they know Brad was working for the CIA? Did they know the prostitute in the seat next to them was an informant? Were they even curious beyond where the day took them? What is crystal clear is all three were like outlaws in a Warren Zevon song.

Once on the ground, Brad, Daddy and Delores were greeted by Guatemalan officials. They stood in a circle with armed and suited men who immediately gifted them Taser guns. It was the late seventies and the black handgun filled with a deadly amount of electricity was a novel sight. Dirt swirled under their feet and wind blew tiny particles of dust into their eyes and teeth. One officer decided to show off the new weapon to his American visitors by shocking his fellow policeman. Poor guy fell to the ground in convulsions. The Guatemalan higher ups all laughed.

"Did Daddy know what was behind that mission?" I asked Uncle Brad. "Did he think of it as dangerous or was he just along for the ride?"

"What do you mean?" Uncle Brad reacted defensively. "Your dad didn't know anything, honey. I'm sure he suspected things but as far as details, he knew no details. And the people involved, as far as I'm concerned, wouldn't want him to know the details. You know, there is no advantage of him knowing the details. I'm sure your dad suspected things…"

Joseph Daniel Chandler was razor-sharp and incredibly intuitive. My father liked to play the country bumpkin, just in for the party, but he knew what was going on around him. I asked Gene Ganucheau, who was heavy in the mix, what his impression of Uncle Brad was. "I just remember your dad talking about Brad working for the government," Gene told me. "That's all I knew. I didn't know it was the CIA. But then he also was working for Jimmy as a bodyguard."

Daddy had a distinct vantage point as it pertained to the bigger picture; well-connected and well-versed in politics and military matters due to my grandfather. Pappy was on the Military Affairs Committee of the U.S. Senate during WWII. He traveled with a group of senators to all the theatres during the war, witnessing gargantuan displays of power. Happy Chandler met with MacArthur and Stillwell among others, recounting their personalities, convictions, and greatest lessons to his youngest son, Dan.

Even through a haze of dazzling entertainment, booze, pot, and cocaine, when his brother-in-law, the former Marine who had also taken over a Philadelphia waste company from Biff Halloran showed up, no way was Daddy completely clueless. "Dan said it around the time when Jimmy was doing all his big gambling," Gene repeated Daddy's comment about Uncle Brad working for the government. "I thought for sure Brad was just a bodyguard, and I knew he was related to your dad in some way, but I didn't know how."

Whether Brad pulled the wool over Dan Chandler's eyes is unclear. What we do know is that long ago meeting at a motel outside of Cincinnati with Drew and the CIA, prompted the probe of drugs in Lexington, morphed into gathering intel about Jimmy Chagra and transmuted into this new mission in Guatemala.

"Did it continue to be about the war on drugs?" I questioned Uncle Brad about how he ended up on Guatemalan soil with Daddy and Delores.

"That was part of it," he said. "That and they were trying to get to certain people and certain sources of certain things... and uh... yeah it was just one step after another. Of course, they didn't know our mission, our vision. Our mission was to develop connections to each thing, each issue which was... you know, very involved, very complicated. We had to accomplish certain things before we could take the next level, the next step and gain confidence of certain people we were trying to get to know. We had to do certain things to make things happen. Initially there was an opportunity there. We knew the connections were one step in front of the other. Colombia was one situation, but you also had a situation in Guatemala and resources there that enabled us to open this door, we had good contacts with the government."

I imagine the inside of my uncle's brain as a maze, a maze of wires sparking in very, as he says, methodical ways, toward a goal that never ends. I asked if he was in Guatemala to get to know drug runners, again rudimentary in my own investigative centrally intelligent way. The amateur journalist in me was trying to connect the Chagra drug running to the confiscated weaponry that was soon to be found in Brad's hotel room and storage unit.

"Once you got to know the people in Guatemala who greeted you," I posed, "the officials who welcomed you, were you aiming for them to lead you to known drug runners?"

"Well, it was more than that," he forgave my ignorance. "When we got there, we got in with the government... ended up getting the opportunity to look at some property that was available. I brought your dad in there to look at the property and he brought Delores with him, and we just looked at some property and talked to some people there."

There was interest from the powers at Caesar's Palace to open a casino in Guatemala, so my father was indeed on a work assignment to look at property. Whether it was Brad, Caesar's executives, or my father's original idea to place a gambling establishment in Guatemala is anyone's guess. At this point, I was less interested in the potential casino or the drug trafficking than I was in trying to connect these ongoing missions with the massive stockpile of weapons discovered in a warehouse in Lexington, Kentucky in my uncle's name.

"Were you all delivering guns to them?"

"No, we were just looking for resources," Uncle Brad said. "Where it went, we didn't know. Where it was going to go, we didn't know. We had to try to develop a relationship... the whole thing is very complicated, there's no one step, next step, next step. You may take one step and then take fifteen, twenty, fifty steps in the opposite direction... do you know what I mean... before you can go back. It was methodical. We had a resource there, enabled us to look at the property in Guatemala. We had to introduce your father to the people, and we ended up bringing, I don't know how many of them back to Las Vegas so they could get to know everything, see the situation, get entertained, give them some money to spend."

This I could picture clearly. I know full well what being entertained in Las Vegas at that time entailed. I imagine the

Guatemalan representatives' mouths dropped as they entered their Caesar's Palace suite, saturated in gaudy glamour. A table full of shrimp, caviar, champagne, and fruit would have surely been waiting for them. Their sunken bubble bath would have overlooked the awesome, dazzling spectacle of shimmering lights in the middle of the desert. I could see the group in full military garb sitting stage side for Wayne Newton, watching spellbound as the American Indian in a bedazzled one-piece swung his microphone 365 degrees before landing it back in his hand and doing a karate kick. Daddy would have been hopped up on booze and excitement, entertaining the group after the show, laughing and telling jokes over dinner at the Ah So.

It was a carnival for Daddy and Delores. "Pretty much, pretty much," Uncle Brad agreed. I doubt they had any idea there were other CIA agents in the country at the same time. The mission was to look at property and get permission to open up a casino. At the same time, Brad and his handlers were putting in groundwork for something else. I wondered how they communicated, if he got his orders from a note inserted in a book in the local library or a phone call to an abandoned pay phone. He was vague on the subject.

"We had resources there we communicated with directly that told us what to do, what not to do and that introduced us to the people," he explained obliquely.

"Other CIA operatives were in Guatemala at the same time?"

"Yes," he confirmed. "Yes. Yep."

My mind's eye watched a thin fellow in his thirties under a palm tree, handsome, blonde hair, loose fitting button down. He stood several yards away from Brad, Daddy, Delores, and the circle of officials joking around with Taser guns. The lone guy seemed to me conspicuously American but didn't draw attention. He patiently waited for the right time to 'communicate.'

According to Brad, the other agents on the ground were not altogether on the same page. "They didn't know what was going on," he said. "They were there just to get to know things, that's all. They didn't know what we were doing other than we were interested in opening up a casino there in Guatemala, possibly."

My uncle was uncomfortable talking about what exactly happened on the ground. He wouldn't give specifics, but apparently, they came upon intelligence that a woman in Nicaragua was doing very bad things, trafficking children chief among them. This became another mission Brad fulfilled for the CIA.

Maybe this woman was the primary goal of the whole 'looking at casino property' exercise. I had to use my imagination. The most violent events are always left unspoken. While pressing for a full visual, I was met with silence. I respected my uncle's privacy and went forward with what seemed a less invasive line of questioning.

"You got the information you needed from the Guatemalan officials to get beyond them… and then they told you about the woman in Nicaragua?"

"No, it was just a link, just a link," he said mysteriously. "We found out about the woman in Nicaragua eventually and it evolved into that."

I visualize pure evil with dark hair and black eyes living in the jungle like a female villain from a David Lynch film. She stands, cigarillo in hand, behind a screen next to a window. Colorful, screaming birds make their way around low hanging tropical trees. A green iguana slithers on the concrete below and like Cruella de Ville, the woman plots her next slaughter. I pull up images on the internet of Nicaraguan political prisoners rotting in jail cells in the center of town. Bars open to the street. People look in as they shop for bread and fruit.

I wondered if Uncle Brad knew when he flew into Central America under the auspices of opening a casino that it would develop into multiple missions. Perhaps it evolved after they had flown back from entertaining the officials in Vegas, so he stood even better connected.

"Nicaraguan jungles… what was that like?" I asked with all of this in mind. "Did the government train you to deal with that situation?"

"Oh yeah, we had to train for it," Uncle Brad affirmed. "We had to find out what we were dealing with, then we had to prepare for it. We went through a lot of training once we eventually found out… we went through a lot of training to prepare for it."

Prepare for it. My imagination took me to an outdoor bar, no… it's a private home, a thatched roof kind of place, made into a mafioso worthy penthouse. Uncle Brad moves in with a few other guys, climbing a set of dark stairs to find the woman in her mid-forties by a window. The woman's eye catches my uncle from the side. This Nicaraguan villain of my own invention turns, a half-smile reveals a missing tooth. She fancies herself a glamorous queen. She doesn't yet know what's happening.

I wondered if Uncle Brad would confirm the images I conjured. Who did they think he was? They had no idea. Perhaps he approached her like a customer of whatever she sold, drugs, guns, little girls. I wondered if he and his associates angled to gain the trust of the people in the room. They did not.

"Naw," he said. "It was too late for that. No, once we went in, that was it. We didn't know that at the time but that was it. That step."

Brad had become completely absorbed in the endless unfolding missions. There were so many things going in so many directions simultaneously, all in service of an invisible goal that was never fully clear to the soldier. Get rid of really bad people doing really bad things. You must get to this individual to get to this individual to gain the confidence of this individual. I am baffled he had the energy to pull off such a life. Yet, Uncle Brad was made for this kind of operation, groomed and programed to follow orders since he was a teenager. Our government knows exactly how to get military or ex-military men to find out about dark goings on in Nicaragua. The CIA knows full well how to train a former marine to get beyond Guatemalan officials to discover deeper issues in question. Bradley Bryant was their man… until he wasn't.

There is no denying these were dark times. "Oh, they were dark," Uncle Brad confirmed. When I asked if he was ever shot, he sounded relieved, even surprised, "No, I was never shot. Nope. No. Thank God. There was a lot of stuff going on down there. Every time you do something like that, you never know… you never know."

Things happen. They always assumed that things could happen. There were back up plans, precautions in place if something like that was to occur. When asked how he went headfirst and determined into such a shadowy enterprise, my uncle intimated he had graduated to the next level, and by which, crossed a point of no return. Navigating through countless levels of danger, he remained patient and focused, "Frankly, you could not let anybody think there was anything on your mind other than that you are totally relaxed."

I see Bradley Bryant, my handsome uncle, on those streets in his thirties, lean and lithe, stony and serious in a brown leather jacket and boots, cooler than any movie star. It's hard to imagine Brad didn't have women falling all over themselves in whatever country he was in, whatever language they spoke. He was the definition of a strong silent type. There was no hair and make-up trailer in Colombia, Nicaragua or Guatemala, no stylist in the wings. I've heard it said you can make a cowboy an actor, but you can't make an actor a cowboy. Uncle Brad was a cowboy, brave and unafraid to die. Match that with the innate charm that might exude from any boy raised by a beautiful, intellectual mother and a rebellious, musician father and you have a force to be reckoned with.

I asked Uncle Brad about his personal life during this spy game, wondering if he had any other relationships at the time, romantic relationships. I pictured young Brad at an outdoor bar in Mexico or Colombia, a few roughed up fellow agents or smugglers, as the case might have been, at his side, pointing out some dark beauty. I can see a high-ranking officer in full military regalia taking him to a late-night soiree filled with gorgeous ladies with long silky auburn hair in those barely-there dresses of the 1970s.

"Did you ever meet anyone you were attracted to?" I asked.

"Uhhhh what was that question?" Uncle Brad smiled. He was shy, almost embarrassed, always reserved when it came to matters of romance or any subject regarding women.

"Did you meet anybody that you really cared about in another country?" I pressed.

"No," he said definitively. "No. No, I couldn't get involved in anything like that." I assumed people tried to set him up. "Oh sure," he said. "Sure. That's always the case, people trying to introduce people and stuff like that." There are as many women deep into the underworld as men. The easiest way to spy on the handsome young American would be from his hotel room. "I can't be involved in that. You can't even think about it... Oh ho, yeah," Uncle Brad chuckled, "Jesus Christ."

Erin Chandler

FIFTEEN

Death of a Gentleman

One sunny Sunday afternoon in El Paso, two days before Christmas 1978, our friend Lee Chagra was murdered. He was shot dead in his office, sitting behind his desk. I was stunned when my father told me the news. It was unimaginable such a tragedy could befall the tight knit siblings who idolized their father. Chan was only fifteen when he flew to El Paso to be at his best friend, Leader's side to comfort him at his father's funeral. Leader and his sisters stood on a platform in front of the crowd of mourners and sang, "(I Would Give) Everything I Own," by Bread. The heartbreaking image stayed with me. Every time that song comes on, I see the beautiful family singing to their beloved patriarch.

Daddy, Chan and I had the emotional reaction most people have when a close member of their inner circle passes. This was a far cry from what Uncle Brad experienced on his end of the equation. "Well, when that happened," Brad said when I asked, "when Lee was killed, Jimmy asked us to come down, go to the... where Lee was being cared for after his murder. We went down and examined the body to see if we could find out... we were trying to find out who did it. After that we stayed back."

This was another jolt of information that didn't sit well as Uncle Brad pried my eyes open with his revelations of what was going on behind the scenes. Now added to that peaceful, loving and heretofore lone image of the five doe-eyed siblings singing in their 1970s attire, long brown hair flowing, I have Uncle Brad in the back room of a cold mortuary. Lee on a silver slab, three men, Brad being one, examining his stiff corpse. Still, instead of Lee naked with a white sheet, as I know he must have been, I picture him lying flat on that silver slab dressed as I always saw him, in a white three-piece suit, bolo tie, gold rings on his fingers and a "FREEDOM" bracelet on his dark wrist.

"When you say 'we,'" I asked Uncle Brad, "who did you go down to El Paso with?"

"Myself and a couple other people," he said cautiously.

"You must have been hardened," I struggled to find a more delicate way to put it, "by this point, to examine the dead body of someone you knew so well. How many years had you been doing things like this without being emotionally attached? I don't know if you were close to Lee..."

"No, no, I wasn't close to Lee," Brad said. "I knew him and that was it. That was it. Honey, we couldn't afford to get close to anybody, from that standpoint, I mean emotionally, you know, outside of family."

I asked if he found out who killed Lee. He did.

Oscar Goodman was Lee Chagra's adoring attorney so I was sure he must have thoroughly investigated the details. "It was two fellas that really had nothing to do with anything," Mr. Goodman said when I asked who committed the murder. "But a robbery it looked like. They robbed him on a weekend. It was a few guys from the military base down there. I don't think they had any connection with anything as it turned out... just plain rotten robbers who turned murderers."

Upon further examination I found out it was exactly that, rotten robbers turned murderers. It was two soldiers, aged twenty and twenty-one from nearby Fort Bliss. Lee had been set up by a distant family member a few days before Christmas. That was the only reason he was at his office on that Sunday afternoon. Simone Taylor, Lee's mother's sister was pure evil. Taylor got together with a guy named Lou Aspor and they developed a plan to rob her nephew, Lee. They found two young soldiers at the military base and convinced them to commit the crime. In court transcripts, the young men said they were told Lee Chagra was an old man with a weak heart who kept money in his boots and all over his office. Simone told them they could probably scare him into submission. Imagine their shock when a handsome thirty-nine-year-old lawyer in a white suit sat behind the desk. Lee tried to reason with the anxious burglars. He said he was a father and husband. Lee told the armed men they could tie him up and take whatever they wanted. Chagra was a smoker and according to the transcripts, they believe that Lee took his Dunhill lighter and tried to light a cigarette and the soldiers thought he was pulling a gun and shot him where he sat. They found a half-lit cigarette in the pool of blood next to Lee.

The death of Lee Chagra marked the end of an era. I venture to say the security and comfort Lee offered during his lifetime held the family's trajectory in place. The absence of his council and protection seemed too big a hole to fill, too great for the family to continue on as before.

"Lee was being harassed by this guy called Judge John H. Wood," Oscar Goodman said of his introduction to the El Paso attorney. "Many of the cases that Lee had were involving alleged drug violations. We were at the Kentucky Derby one year, your dad was with us, Lee came up to me and he says, 'you know I think I'm going to call you and talk to you about the situation that I have with this judge.' Then Lee called and we were considering a civil rights complaint against the judge. The judge absolutely was hurting Lee's law practice because people would stop going to him if they knew the judge was going to be sitting because he was going to give them the maximum."

A few months after Lee's murder, Jimmy Chagra was slated to appear before 'Maximum John' in a Texas court to be sentenced for drug trafficking violations. The magistrate earned this nickname because, as Oscar indicated, he was infamous for handing down the harshest sentences for drug dealers. In San Antonio on May 29th, 1979, Judge John H. Wood was gunned down. Wood was the first federal judge to be assassinated in the United States. The hired killer was Charles Harrelson, a regular from that seedy Las

Vegas scene of the moment. The gunman who knew all the players, including the Chagras, was the father of actor Woody Harrelson.

The high flying Chagra family empire came tumbling down. This assassination landed two of Lee's brothers, Jimmy and Joe, as well as his sister-in-law, in prison. In December of 1982, a Texas jury convicted Jimmy Chagra's wife, Elizabeth, of paying Charles Harrelson $250,000.00 to kill Judge Wood. Jimmy Chagra himself was never convicted of the murder for hire, thanks to a flashy turn by Oscar Goodman who convinced the jury there was reasonable doubt.

They eventually found Jimmy guilty of tax evasion and drug trafficking and he went to federal prison. Author of *Strength of the Pack: The Personalities, Politics and Espionage Intrigues that Shaped the DEA*, Douglas Valentine, shed light on the subject over a recorded Zoom conversation. He explained to me the chain of events that landed Lee and Jimmy Chagra on the Fed's most wanted list.

"In 1971 they started what was called Operation Sandstone and this was the big investigation that swept up the Chagras," Doug Valentine said. "They found out that Lee Chagra down in El Paso through his Syrian and Lebanese relatives in Mexico was receiving marijuana and cocaine. Lee was called the Black Striker. He was a character. He's the one who initially dipped the toe in the waters that dragged the whole family down... I knew that Brad was in Philadelphia and was part of it."

PART III

THE FALL

Erin Chandler

CHAPTER
SIXTEEN

Bluegrass Conspiracy?

"I'm one of the good guys," Uncle Brad said to the officer placing him in handcuffs. Bradley Fred Bryant, my beautiful uncle, was finally set free. In an instant, he was excavated from the razor's edge while waiting to board a plane at the Airport Sheridan in Philadelphia. It was 1980. This new 'handler' took immediate possession of Brad's bronze leather briefcase and found twenty-two thousand dollars cash and a handful of fake ID's and passports. His case was filled with semi-automatic weapons and silencers, there was a ski mask, a commando dagger, Russian-English and Spanish-English dictionaries, and top secret coding equipment of the United States government. Perhaps most damning was the key to a storage unit in Lexington, Kentucky, where a stolen cannon from the China Lake Military Naval Center was soon found, sealing his fate toward a different type of captivity.

On the heels of Brad's arrest, his childhood friend and business partner, Andrew Carter Thornton, an expert paratrooper turned cop, turned lawyer, turned drug trafficker, met his end when he jumped from a private plane above Knoxville, Tennessee. Attached to his faulty parachute was a similar cache of knives and guns, forty-five hundred dollars cash and a duffel bag holding forty kilos of cocaine.

Brad Bryant and Drew Thornton were still in their thirties. The bluegrass sons were well-bred, well-trained, well-armed and mythologized by sensational reporting that chalked them up to spoiled country club socialites who became international drug dealers. In 2023, the Hollywood movie *Cocaine Bear* turned Drew Thornton's tragic end into a punch line. All a stranger's staging of my mom's younger brother and his best friend, a visitor's perception of Lexington, Kentucky, a narrative aimed for those outside the velvet rope to swallow up in one ill-informed gulp. To assume Uncle Brad and Drew were ne'er do well rich kids who turned privilege and connections into drug trading, greed, and murder, is to ignore a militarized society that has irrevocably changed the course of many young men's lives. Getting down the bitter pill that their work began under the direction of a private sector of our United States government goes against our insatiable need to create a villain. We don't want our illusions shattered by muddying the waters with sticky details of sanctioned military behavior beyond our wildest dreams.

CHAPTER
SEVENTEEN

"This was a James Bond sort of story, an amazing story. There's something awfully strange here."

—US Attorney Peter F. Vaira

Routine Arrest Uncovers Web of Global Intrigue:
UPI Archives December 8th, 1980
(in part)

PHILADELPHIA—A routine bust last January has led federal authorities on a probe of a clandestine web of drug smuggling, global intrigue and thefts of military hardware with shadowy CIA connections.

One of three men arrested last Jan. 4 is believed to be a high-ranking associate of a nationwide group of mercenaries and drug-smugglers called 'The Company', which has reportedly handled $55 million worth of drugs, The (Philadelphia) Bulletin said in a copyright story Sunday.

Bradley F. Bryant, 36, the reputed member of The Company, also allegedly did contract work for the CIA and was reportedly involved in the theft of U.S. military weapons that were to be swapped in Libya for sophisticated Russian radar.

Bryant's cousin, former Air Force officer, Larry Earl Bryant, 40, also is under investigation in connection with thefts of equipment from a secret naval ordnance station at China Lake, Calif., which occurred over a period of several years.

The paper quoted federal sources as saying Larry Bryant told them his cousin and another man were involved in stealing Russian radar in Libya for the CIA. Bryant denied making the statement.

"This was a James Bond sort of story, an amazing story," said U.S. Attorney, Peter F. Vaira, recalling the arrests last winter. ' "There's something awfully strange here."

Philadelphia police, who thought they were investigating routine drug smuggling, arrested the Bryants and a third man, Roger Barnard, 30, at the Philadelphia International Airport.

But when officers picked up Bradley Bryant, they found no drugs. Instead, police said they found semi-automatic weapons, sophisticated coding equipment, $22,800 cash, 10 counterfeit Kentucky driver's licenses and a semi-automatic pistol.

Baggage confiscated from Larry Bryant and Barnard at a hotel near the airport turned up pistols, commando daggers, a silencer, ski masks, ammunition, disguises and 11 phony driver's licenses.

Hotel managers tipped off police to Larry Bryant and Barnard when the pair aroused suspicions by paying for their rooms with $100 bills.

Police also found a pamphlet entitled 'The Top-Secret Radio Frequencies of the United States Government'; Russian-English and Spanish-English dictionaries, and stationery listing the

address and work habits of a man named George Haddad --
described by sources as an agent who has done intelligence-
related work for the United States and Libya.

Since then, Larry Bryant has been acquitted of charges of
possessing a silencer. His cousin and Barnard are awaiting trial
in Philadelphia.

Bradley Bryant, of Lexington, Ky., also has alleged
connections to a high-rolling narcotics smuggler considered a
suspect in the 1979 killing of a federal judge in Texas.

In 1979, a former suburban Philadelphia businessman had a
contract to provide 'bodyguard' services for Jimmy Chagra, a
convicted El Paso, Texas, drug smuggler, the newspaper quotes
sources as saying. Chagra is a suspect in the May 29, 1979
assassination of U.S. District Judge John Wood, who was to
preside over a drug hearing involving Chagra.

Worry Over Illegal Exports Growing Among
U.S. Prosecutors
Phillip Taubman, Special to the New York Times
July 1981
(in part)

Also charged with receipt of embezzled Government property in
the case are Larry E. Bryant, a retired Air Force electronics expert,
and his cousin, Bradley F. Bryant.

When he was first questioned about the missing equipment,
according to investigative reports prepared by the Bureau of
Alcohol, Tobacco and Firearms, Mr. Nichols explained that he
had removed the equipment as the first step in a complex plan,
sponsored by the C.I.A., to trade military equipment in Libya for a
piece of Soviet radar equipment.

According to officials at China Lake, the center has, on occasion,
been supplied with Soviet radar equipment in order to test
countermeasures. Officials say they do not know, and do not ask,
how the Soviet equipment is obtained.

The Federal Bureau of Investigation traced some of the night scopes, used to aim weapons at night through infrared detection, to Las Vegas, where agents observed them being transported by Larry Bryant in a car.

In an interview in Las Vegas last week, Larry Bryant said that he did not know that the cartons he was transporting contained night scopes. Mr. Bryant said that while stationed at Nellis Air Force Base near Las Vegas, he had made occasional trips to China Lake to assist in research projects. Officials at the center said that Mr. Bryant had worked closely at the center with Mr. Calvani.

Arrests in Philadelphia

On Jan. 4, 1980, while the disappearance of the night scopes and other equipment was under investigation in California and Nevada, the Philadelphia police arrested Bradley and Larry Bryant at an airport hotel. The pair were being watched in a routine vice investigation, and the police said that they found a small cache of arms in Bradley Bryant's suitcases.

According to the Philadelphia police and Federal investigators, both Bryants told the authorities that they were working for an unspecified government agency. Larry Bryant, these officials said, told officers that the guns were part of a plan to trade weapons in Libya for Soviet radar equipment and that the project was authorized by the C.I.A.

Larry Bryant, in an interview, said that story was a garbled version of what he had told the police. He said that he had told them that he had specialized in electronic warfare in the Air Force and knew a lot about Soviet radar and that he might also have mentioned discussions in the early 1970s among his colleagues in the Air Force about a plan to swap American military equipment in Libya for an important piece of Soviet radar equipment. The plan was never carried out, he said.

The Philadelphia police, he said, had twisted these separate stories into one story. After the acquittal of Larry Bryant on charges of illegal possession of a silencer and the conviction of Bradley Bryant on the same charge, the reported C.I.A. connection was raised anew at the April 1981 sentencing hearing.

Alleged C.I.A. Contract

Assistant United States Attorney Steven Weiner testified that Bradley Bryant claimed that "he was under C.I.A. contract during the time" of his arrest. Mr. Bryant's lawyer, Oscar Goodman, said his client had not said he had a contract with the C.I.A., but had told prosecutors of a contract with an unnamed government agency.

Mr. Goodman, in an interview, said that the issue of Bradley Bryant's possible relationship with the C.I.A. was a confidential matter covered by lawyer-client privilege.

The C.I.A. denied at the time, and still does, that any of the figures in the stolen-hardware case from China Lake had connections with the agency.

The arrests in Philadelphia led to the search of a warehouse in Lexington rented by Bradley Bryant where police found a large arsenal of weapons valued at more than $250,000, various electronic surveillance devices and an infrared night scope. Federal authorities believe that the night scope found in Lexington was one of the 10 from China Lake.

Larry Bryant was not charged in Lexington. Bradley Bryant was acquitted there in May 1980 on a charge of illegal possession of firearms.

On May 20 of this year, Bradley Bryant was arrested in Illinois and charged with unlawful delivery of 804 pounds of marijuana to federal undercover agents. He is currently being held in prison in Elgin, Ill.

Bartering for Weapons

Federal authorities who are familiar with these cases said that they believed the hardware stolen from China Lake was actually intended for use in exchange for drugs in Colombia. They discount the possibility that either Larry Bryant or Bradley Bryant or the two civilians from the weapons center seriously hoped to swap the hardware and weapons in Libya.

But sources in the Defense Department said that at the time the equipment was removed from China Lake, Government agents covertly acquiring Soviet electronic weapons systems often resorted to bartering American military equipment in third-party nations such as Libya.

Bluegrass Sons

Erin Chandler

CHAPTER

EIGHTEEN

"Your secrets are your life."

—Bradley Bryant

With the floodgates burst open, it was anyone's guess how deep and wide it all went. News outlets and journalists scrambled to find out where Bradley Bryant, Larry Bryant and Drew Thornton stood in the larger picture of international drug smuggling and arms trading. Everyone had their own theory of how the CIA and other private sectors of our United States government were involved with these former military men.

"I was arrested originally in Philadelphia," Uncle Brad explained in a soft, relaxed tone about his first arrest at the airport on January 4th, 1980. "Initially it was because a girl that worked for me as an executive assistant had been married at some point to a DEA agent that she had broken up with. I want to say he was behind it. I was staying at a hotel at the airport, I had gone in to visit my kids. My wife and I were separated at the time, I had gone in to see my kids and I was getting ready to leave. At the same time, I had a meeting. I had a meeting with some other people there and they ended up arresting me at the airport."

I couldn't help but notice Brad's calm talking about the arrest. It sounded like his runaway train screeching to a halt was relatively painless. He mentioned that his sister-in-law had made a comment that he was a 'walking heart attack' at just thirty-five years old. His stress level was palpable as he moved between the world of secret agent/drug smuggler and family/businessman. I imagine it was a tremendous relief when it was finally over. How on earth could it not have been? The secrecy, deceiving those he loved, endless orders from good and bad actors alike, and constant traveling from one third world country to another, was over.

Brad and his cousin Larry Bryant, who was also arrested, were reportedly being followed in a routine vice investigation. Uncle Brad went on to tell me that his 'associate' was having a relationship with a security guard's wife at the Philadelphia hotel. "Yeah, hard to believe but he did," Brad exhaled, "some nonsense."

Enter again three-time Las Vegas mayor, Oscar Goodman. The famed criminal defense attorney came to the table this time in no small part due to Dear, my irrepressible grandmother, Angelee Bradley Bryant. At the behest of Dan Chandler, her former son in law, Dear flew to Las Vegas to meet with Goodman. She was in regular contact with Daddy even after the divorce. She adored him and he was the one in the family with connections to powerful lawyers. Phone lines buzzed between Mamma, Dear, Daddy Gene, Aunt Leigh, and Uncle Earl about how they could help Brad. Springing into action, Dear took up the fight like a champ and in an instant. I've heard it said if you're in trouble and need something done, don't call the cops, call a mother.

"Mrs. Chick was the classiest woman who ever came to my office," Oscar Goodman said buoyantly. Dear was living in Pinehurst, North Carolina and married to William Chick, hence taking the name Angelee Bryant Chick. "Mrs. Chick came out and met with me, I said... and this is the truth... I said to myself, this guy can't be guilty of anything having a mother as nice as this lady!"

Angelee Bryant Chick 'Dear'

Dear would have been a great mobster's moll with her southern charm and worldly wit, her porcelain skin and classic beauty, angel fine blonde curls, silk pastel tops with soft bows and pleated skirts over sheer pantyhose, and of course high heels. Angelee was a woman to be reckoned with. She wasn't the least bit fazed by anything or anyone when it came to protecting her first-born son, Bradley.

"I like Brad very much," Oscar began, agreeing to a recorded interview in late 2021. "Brad was a stand-up guy. He was a very smart guy and he played everything very close to the vest, even with me. And it was a tough case... I'd like to start backwards. I'd like to start with the trial and the fact that unfortunately after I made my closing argument, I got an order in effect from a judge in Kansas City that a jury was going to be selected and I better be there representing my client. I had to leave and I put Brad in the hands of a very competent young lady who was my co-council. She ultimately became the mayor of Lexington. Shortly after the trial, I flew to Kansas City and began the jury selection. There was a note that was handed to me by the bailiff I couldn't believe. I sort of let out a 'Whoopee!' in the middle of the jury selection! Everyone looked at me like I was crazy because it said, 'you just got a not guilty in the Kentucky case.' I was so happy. I was happy for a million different reasons..."

Brad was charged with possession of an illegal weapon. They had evidence that he was renting a storage unit in which they found the cannon that was the subject of the charge. "Fifty mm cannon and your uncle's fingerprints were, if I recall, on the lot as well as on the gun..." Oscar explained. "So, it was very difficult to get a verdict, but the jury came in and I'm happy for your uncle and I'm happy for your grandmother and I was happy for myself at the time. Mrs. Chick, she's the best. I love her. If I ever got into trouble, I would want Angelee Chick on my side."

Fascination grew as news of the surprising arrests of the Pennsylvania businessman from Kentucky and his cousin Larry flooded the airwaves. Journalist Phillip Taubman revealed in the *New York Times* in July of 1981, an international web of secrecy involving illegal exporting of arms and sophisticated radar equipment from the Soviet Union to Libya. When writing about the theft at the China Lake Naval Base, he pointed at two former Central Intelligence agents, Edwin C. Wilson and Francis E. Terpil who were indicted for trying to send explosives to terrorist training camps. Employees of the Naval Weapons Center were found to have traveled to Libya to educate terrorist as to how to use the explosives. Phillip Taubman reported in the same article about Brad and Larry Bryant and their 'associate' Ralph (aka Pete) Calvani.

On May 20th, 1981, Uncle Brad was arrested again in Illinois, charged with unlawful delivery of 804 pounds of marijuana to federal undercover agents. Brad and Larry's associate, Pete Calvani lured Brad to a hotel for the sting. Calvani initiated a marijuana transportation deal and then communicated with authorities what was expected. Brad was taken into custody on the spot.

"He set it up and that was it…" Uncle Brad's voice trailed off remembering, "and the rest… one step after another."

I asked if this was related to Jimmy Chagra's smuggling operation, Brad told me he had advanced beyond Jimmy as far as resources and material. Slowly but surely, Brad

Erin Chandler

was cracking case after case, uncovering his next move and
advancing to the next level. "I mean it's complicated," he
said. "I mean Jesus…"

I wondered what the process was in the event of
exposure and capture, what protocol was set into motion.
As an undercover associate with the CIA, what protection
was offered?

"At the time you don't know," Uncle Brad explained. "You
think you're protected, or you assume you're protected and
that certain things will happen, but you have to understand
that you can't really step out of the darkness and expect… you
know, what happens to the people that are protecting you?
They're providing everything to start with so if they step out,
you kind of destroy the whole program, the whole situation."

I conveyed my obstinate bewilderment concerning the
culture of disavowing, private sectors of government turning
their backs and in a very real sense, leaving a man behind.
"I'm trying to understand how you would not be protected
at all by the CIA," I beat the dead horse. "The informant, or
turned informant, who turned you in, he is not on the same
page? The DEA is not on the same page as the CIA?"

"Oh no," Uncle Brad said adamantly. "Hell no. No.
They had no idea. They don't know. They don't know. They
can't know. In the back of your mind, you think there's
communication but there can't be because you wouldn't
know who to trust there."

Brad went out on a limb as a drug trafficker to get
information on the Chagras before stepping further into the
"darkness" when tasked to find out who was beyond that
person, then further when they wanted to know who was
beyond them. It was a never-ending mission with no proposed

144

conclusion to Bradley Bryant's undercover identities and ongoing duty. It would have been an act of God to continue that way and not be eventually found out. When the inevitable unfolded, he was out of luck but not bewildered. His sense of patriotism was so deeply ingrained he remained silent and dutiful regardless of personal consequences.

"You have to know at the beginning, you're on your own," Brad affirms the unfathomable. "This is what we're trying to accomplish. This is the mission and basically assume your lies are your life. My secrets are my life."

Erin Chandler

CHAPTER
NINETEEN

The Chicago Lawyer

O nce again, Dear flew into action, this time with my mom, Lynne, in tow. Brad's mother and sister arrived at a hotel room in Chicago and began searching for legal help. They immediately discovered a well-respected lawyer named Fred Morelli. The handsome criminal defense attorney with a gentle manner, dark hair and dark eyes had a remarkable understanding of the law as he had been a part-time public defender since 1967 and a judge from 1976 to 1981. When my mother first called, Fred wasn't interested in the case. Desperate to convince him, she put Dear on the phone. Thankfully, the charm of Angelee Bryant Chick resonated, and he met with them that very afternoon. After a few hours with Brad Bryant's gracious, and graceful family, Fred Morelli agreed to be his lawyer.

"I remember most of the case like it was yesterday," recalled Mr. Morelli when we spoke in 2021. "I remember going to meet Brad at the Kane County jail. I was immediately impressed with him. He was charged with possession with intent to deliver 804 pounds of marijuana. A guy named Pete Calvani had given him up. I don't know why Calvani gave him up. I don't remember off the top of my head why but the way that usually works is somebody gets arrested, and the cops say, 'well, you know what you can do to help yourself?' And they give up their best friend."

Fred Morelli uncovered evidence connecting Uncle Brad to the CIA. It was his recollection that they were trying to get money together to steal a Russian radar from Libya. It was a clandestine operation and there would be no public money to fund this so Mr. Morelli concluded it was the CIA that put Brad in the marijuana business to fund getting this Russian radar out of Libya. He was able to establish in court Brad's involvement with the CIA even though he was disavowed, as is common practice if a soldier is working undercover. Nevertheless, it was hard to ignore the connection Fred Morelli established via a photograph taken of Brad Bryant at a Super Bowl game seated right next to the head of the Central Intelligence Agency.

"I was able to establish that Brad sat next to the Director of the CIA for the Western United States or the West Coast, I don't remember which, at a Super Bowl game," Fred told me. "Now you don't just happen that your ticket is right next to the head of the CIA, right? You know, that doesn't happen by accident. When I would contact the CIA to try to get any kind of confirmation, the only thing that I could get back from them was, 'We have searched our data base, and we have no record of the individual you mentioned.' I've seen that exact language since then. I mean word for word. They must press a button on the typewriter and that whole sentence comes out."

My mom recalls Dear's documents of proof, a piece of paper with code names and numbers and letters that Brad had given to my grandmother in case anything happened to him. These, he said, would verify his work with the government.

A podcast called *The Real Narcos* by Nosier told the story of Barry Seal. In one episode, they discussed pilot Barry Seal from Baton Rouge, Louisiana who was in the smuggling business. While the stories and motives are different, the methods, time frame and government interaction are alike. Bradley Bryant was similar to Barry Seal in that he was in touch with the government while smuggling drugs from Colombia in the late seventies. He was dissimilar in that Barry turned informant after his arrest. Brad was working for the government from the beginning and when arrested went mute.

Fred Morelli was convinced and determined to persuade the jury that Bradley Bryant was not simply a drug trafficker, it went much deeper. "Because my impression of him was that he was bigger than that," Fred explained. "You know, I've represented lots of drug dealers from the guy on the street corner to people flying DC-3 loads across the Caribbean and Brad just seemed bigger than all that. It seemed to me that he had way more going for him than being a drug dealer. Too smart. Too well connected. Too well educated. Too well spoken. And he didn't seem… some drug dealers, I think are addicted to adrenalin and after they've got enough money out of it, they do it for the rush. But that didn't seem to be Brad at all either."

During Fred's long representation of my uncle, he himself was surveilled. One of his clients worked for the phone company and informed him that his phone was bugged. Fred pointed out that it was much more difficult to get such a thing ordered back in the 1970s and 1980s than it is in 2022. He knew it was the government and has since conducted himself as if his phone is always bugged.

I asked about Brad and Drew's lifelong connection, the Sewanee Military Academy, and that fateful motel off the interstate in Cincinnati where my uncle met with the CIA for the first time. "I remember Brad talking about Drew," Fred said. "I remember when Drew was killed in a parachuting jump with (what was) supposed to have been 80 pounds of drugs. The thing I remember about Drew's death is that he's coming in on a parachute and he's wearing these real lightweight Italian loafers. That's really about all I know about Drew. I never spoke to him. I never met him. I never really knew what his involvement was. Brad was very closed-mouthed and never volunteered any information about anything. If I asked him a question, he told me the answer. And he knew that if I asked him the question, I needed the truthful answer. But he never volunteered anything. He's not a talker."

In the end, Fred remembers that the judge was kind to Brad but was shocked when he got the sentence. He received fifteen years. According to the parole guidelines, Brad should have been out in three. They wouldn't let him go because they had in custody the only person who could inform on Jimmy Chagra concerning the murder of Judge 'Maximum John' Wood.

Brad was brought in over and over to testify against Chagra. He persistently refused to do so. He would get on the stand, and they would ask him questions and he would refuse to answer. Fred recalls one Texas court where Brad was called to testify. It was the John Wood Memorial Courthouse in the John Wood Memorial Courtroom and there was an oil painting of Judge John Wood. "Well," Fred thought, "this is going to be a lot of fun. I mean the whole thing was geared at getting Brad to… use the slang expression, to roll over on Jimmy Chagra," Fred explained. "You know, Brad really wasn't going to do that. I think he gave it the right amount of thought. He didn't just out of hand reject it, he gave it the proper amount of thought and decided he just wasn't going to do that."

I felt my uncle's frustration all these years later regarding the convoluted world, which once made so much sense, that he occupied decades ago. It seemed important he make clear that he went into the madness, the merry-go-round, the danger, betrayals, lies, the whole shooting match with his eyes wide open. Unfortunately, they will forever remain that way.

"Some things are hard to forget. Yeah, yeah," he laughed morosely. "Jesus Christ, I don't know, doll. I don't want to destroy anybody's life by doing this. A lot of memories kid, a lot of memories… Jesus Christ, a lot of fun!"

The Bryant family: Leigh Bryant Stevenson, Bradley Bryant,
Angelee Bryant Chick, Earl Bryant and Lynne Bryant Chandler

CHAPTER
TWENTY

A Family Affair

After Brad's arrest, the FBI descended on his younger sister, Leigh Bryant Stevenson and her husband, Joel, in Birmingham, Alabama. Uncle Joel had been the chief financial officer of Bryson Enterprise so it was no surprise they would be in hot pursuit to investigate Bradley Bryant's business partners. Aunt Leigh was blind-sided by the allegations. "Well of course I thought it couldn't be true," she said. "That was not the Bradley I knew. There was nothing, no indication, other than him being gone all the time, which is what most high-powered businessmen are, gone all the time… or it seems that way."

This was not the world they grew up in, drug dealers, guns, gangsters, and spies. These were not the circles the gifted and gracious Bryant family embraced. There was no correlation between that world and the loving siblings who grew up singing songs and trying to keep their romantic parents together. This was not on the forefront of Dear's mind when she moved out of their home on Fincastle to a less prestigious neighborhood and began to pick up the pieces as a single mother of four. This was not something that could have been foreseen by Daddy Gene, my World War II veteran and orchestra leader grandfather. This would have been unfathomable to Daddy Fred, my great-grandfather from an impoverished upbringing in Appalachia, who pulled himself up by his bootstraps to create a new life for the Bryants in Lexington. This drama was all seventies. All flash. All greed. All government secrets and callousness. It was a new world none of my forefathers could have predicted would come into play during the third quarter of the twentieth century.

That Brad got away with this secret life, that he was able to keep this darkness separate from his friends and family is extraordinary. He was a master of compartmentalization. His lies were indeed his life.

"When people would show up asking us questions," my uncle, Joel Stevenson, still hot on the subject said, "I would treat them the same way I'm treating you. I don't know what you're talking about! I don't have a clue!" Joel consulted his lawyer when he found out the FBI wanted to pay them a visit. His attorney asked if he had anything to hide. Since he had nothing to hide, he was advised not to force them to get a subpoena and welcome them over. The FBI came and one agent stayed a full week. The man combed through every box and document Aunt Leigh and Uncle Joel had. Joel told his office manager, Garnett Sewell, to get the man anything he wanted and if she couldn't find it, find someone who could. Then they loaded everything onto a truck. By the end of the week, the FBI agent had bonded with my charming uncle.

"The FBI guy, this is no shit Erin," Uncle Joel said, "the FBI guy took his coat off, took his tie off, took his shirt off, he had a t-shirt on, and he helped me load that truck. He said to me… and this is the first time that I had any idea that there was some nefarious… you know I didn't know why Bradley had been arrested. I had no idea! He was in Philadelphia. I'm in fucking Birmingham, okay? He said to me, I never will forget this, guy says, 'you know, this is such a shame Joel. We don't want Bradley. We didn't want him. That's not who we were after. We were after some guy named Chagra.' That was the first time I ever heard Chagra's name."

He must have been shocked at the scene unfolding. Joel Stevenson is anything but a scofflaw. With his brother-in-law/business partner, whom he deeply respected, in custody, I imagine he was both forthcoming and protective. What were his thoughts about this drama happening so close to home? Did it seem comprehensible that Brad could be a spy for the CIA, a drug smuggler, a gun runner? I pressed my uncle on the matter.

"What did I think?" Joel shot back defensively. "I didn't think anything. I didn't think, oh he's a bad guy, oh he shouldn't have been doing that. All I know is whatever he did, whatever he truly did, he paid for in spades. He's paid his fuckin' debt. He doesn't owe anybody anything."

I backed away from this obviously sore spot. Joel Stevenson loves Bradley Bryant, unconditionally and forever. Brad was everything Joel wanted to be as a businessman. He never had a conversation with his brother-in-law about his various side hustles, never assumed he had the right to approach Brad with questions like, 'Hey what did you do for Chagra?' or 'I heard that you were running some marijuana.' Those kinds of conversations never took place. Furthermore, he didn't care. He understood his wife's brother was closed mouth to the extreme and wouldn't have told him anyway, so he just didn't go there.

"Did you ever meet Drew Thornton?" I asked Joel before letting him go.

"I think I met him one time," he said. "We played racquetball together one night as I remember. You know he was a nice guy. I thought he was a policeman. I wasn't sure about that. I wasn't sure if he was a policeman or a lawyer. I didn't know. But anyway we had a nice time. That's the only time I ever saw him."

Bluegrass Sons

Erin Chandler

CHAPTER
TWENTY-ONE

Tinker Tailor Soldier Spy

We went to see Uncle Brad when he was held at a federal penitentiary in Atlanta in 1984. At nineteen, I didn't know why he was incarcerated. I don't recall being alarmed at the circumstances or scared. I just remember being happy to see him. Across the busy prison yard on that windy October day, I spotted Brad approaching in a fitted khaki short-sleeved shirt tucked neatly into matching khaki pants. Head up and smiling, he greeted Mamma, Chan and me at a picnic table in the middle of the fenced-in visiting area.

Stronger than ever was the shining light of my grandmother's eye, the brother my mother and her sister adored, the uncle we referred to behind closed doors as our ace in the hole, if anybody messes with us, Brad'll get 'em!

The Philadelphia judge gave Brad fifteen years and as Fred Morelli pointed out, according to the parole guidelines enforced at the time he should have been out in three. He spent ten years in custody. The FBI wanted intelligence on the Chagras and Brad was their ticket. They threatened him to no avail, attempting to shake out any information he had on the CIA as well as the criminals he dealt with.

Bradley Fred Bryant was tough, silent, and stoic as federal agents moved him an unprecedented one hundred and thirty times. Never unhinged, he focused on working with other prisoners, helping them with their cases. Brad spent hours, days, months, and years at the various prison libraries. When a fellow prisoner was serving more time than they were supposed to, he helped them analyze their cases and make sense of things they wouldn't have otherwise understood. At another prison, he became the chaplain's assistant. Throughout the 1980s, Brad was transported from California to Philadelphia, then Texas and back to California. It was an attempt to break his spirit, which as it turned out was impossible. I asked Fred Morelli why they moved him one hundred and thirty times.

"It was called diesel therapy," Fred said of the frenetic uprooting from prison to prison. "I remember we had a court appearance in California, in Fresno, and I flew out there. It wasn't until I got there that I was told that he had been moved to Philadelphia. Am I gonna throw a temper tantrum? Of course not. As a criminal defense lawyer, you don't get anywhere through temper tantrums. So, you know, you're polite to everybody whether you like 'em or not. You're polite to everybody, and you're cordial and you're friendly. The things that you can't control you recognize, you know, I'm not in control of this."

They don't play by rules we are accustomed to. They don't even pretend to. They were not sure how to handle this incarcerated agent. They couldn't be certain where his loyalties lay and didn't want him to be settled long enough to tell anybody anything. They didn't want Brad's family or associates to know where he was. They didn't count on Angelee Bradley Bryant Chick. Dear knew where he was every minute of every day, every town of every state, every penitentiary, every tiny jail cell.

Lynne Bryant Chandler was also fiercely loyal to her brother. One hot August morning, Mamma and my stepfather, Paul Knipping, drove fifteen hours to Seguin, Texas. They pulled up to what she described as a tiny square block in the middle of the desert, like a Mexican jail out of an old Western movie.

"It was a stone building with bars in the windows," she remembered. "No screens or anything and I literally almost fainted."

When my mom got inside, a large woman with broken teeth and frizzed, dyed red hair with bald patches, ravaged through her purse. "This female officer implied she would like to have some powder, some nice powder just so I could see my brother." Mamma assured the jailer she would return with the powder after she saw Brad. They put her in an empty glass room and slammed the door, locking it behind her. A few minutes later, an armed guard brought my uncle into another glass room facing her. Uncle Brad was rail thin, pale, and rigid as a steel rod. Another officer walked with a rifle behind him, back and forth, back and forth.

They had only spoken for five minutes when a man came abruptly into the room. "Time's up Bryant," he said. Uncle Brad stood up obedient and expressionless, without a glance toward his sister, turned around and walked out. They slammed the door behind him.

Mamma and Paul went to the grocery and got three giant bags of groceries, as well as the requested powder and took it back to the jail. They bought Uncle Brad canned tuna, canned chicken and crackers, anything they thought would be nutritious. Then they drove fifteen hours back to Lubbock where they were living at the time. Ironically, the guards handed Brad the bags without even checking. After the melodramatic display of authority, they could have placed a gun in the bag. Brad gave most of the food away to the people at the jail. He knew they would be moving him again within hours.

Every time he was moved, Brad gathered up his few belongings. He packed everything in a banker's box his attorney gave him which contained his legal papers. The box kept falling apart. Fred eventually taped it together, so it would remain intact. Fred Morelli always traveled with a suit that belonged to Brad so his client could wear it to the next court date in another city.

Like clockwork, Angelee started the whole procedure again. She first called where she thought her son was being held. "I'm sorry," someone would say. "He's been transferred." Dear bulldozed back, called and called and called and called until they had to tell her where he had been moved. My grandmother tracked her son every single day as square-jawed U.S. government agents in black suits moved him, chess-like in precision, from state to state, institution to institution, from a dump of a stucco jail cell in Seguin, Texas to a maximum-security prison in California.

Angelee was a force of nature, researching tirelessly, discovering records and documents of undeniable proof linking Brad to the CIA. She took on an entire government system riddled with inconsistencies as the DEA, CIA and FBI were all decidedly at odds with each other. By the time Brad arrived at the next prison, Fred had been contacted and was ready to take up the fight from there.

"I remember one time I said to Brad, 'Brad does anybody bother you in here?'" Fred Morelli recalled asking his client about any potential danger from fellow prisoners. "He said, 'Fred not only does no one bother me, when I am around no one bothers anyone.' He had an air about him that you didn't want to mess around with him. Brad never had any problems in there, all it took was a withering glance."

Uncle Brad was put in a cell with no bed, no mattress, no toilet and no blanket when it was freezing outside. He got a bad case of bronchitis. They put him into open population and told him there was a contract on him. At another institution, his cell was set on fire. Brad knew he was in danger and the FBI repeated, "if you talk to us about the CIA, tell us about your activities…" Then he was someplace else 24 hours later.

"I remember Bradley calling me from prison and saying that he was thinking seriously about putting his family in protective services," Mamma said. "He considered moving them to protect them because the FBI was threatening him to tell them about what the CIA was involved in and if he didn't, they were going to go after his family. He was afraid of that. They threatened to break his back. I remember that very well."

When Brad was at Lompoc, a maximum security prison in California, the prison guards came to get him out of his cell and told him he had a visitor. He was led out of the prison and into a waiting car. It turned out it was the CIA with Brad's handler.

"I was there, I don't know a week, maybe a few days," Uncle Brad remembered. "They pull me out and I go out and there are a couple cars out there. Course I'm all shackled and stuff like that but I get in the car and they pull down the road. Then they pulled over and took me out and took the shackles off and everything else and this guy I was in contact with climbed in the backseat with me and we talked for a little bit. We stopped at a motel and went in and had a meal. At the end of the table there were five or six guys set at the table next to us. The only thing he really asked me was 'what do you think you're... what are you gonna do?' And my comment was pretty simple, I'm gonna do what I have to do, do my time and hopefully get out of here with some life left and get back to my family. So that was it. They picked me up, dropped me off, took me down the road to a small location down there, I forget what they call it... spent about a week down there at this other location and then they brought me back and transferred me to Chicago. I remember checking in there, they said, the guy said, we thought you escaped," Brad laughed. "Oh yeah, funny, funny."

I asked if he had given a different answer to that question, if he hadn't said he would keep quiet, do his time and get back to his family, if those men might have killed him.

"I think it's a possibility," Uncle Brad said casually. "Yep, yep… yep."

Erin Chandler

CHAPTER
TWENTY-TWO

Strength of the Pack

B est-selling author, Douglas Valentine, *CIA and Organized Crime: How Illegal Operations Corrupt America and the World,* has spent his life publishing books on the CIA. With his extensive research and knowledge, I asked what he would call my uncle in relation to the government agency. Doug explained the hierarchy. There are CIA officers who are fully integrated backstop employees of the CIA. They have their own civil service contract set up. They get insurance, a pension when they retire, and are fully protected. Then there are contract agents, people who sign on the dotted line that they are going to work for the CIA for a while. He said a lot of military people are contract agents, or they might be the PLO, Palestinian and Liberation Organization, or some banker in Switzerland. These guys or girls do contract work for them, and they receive money for doing that, or aid in kind. Sometimes the CIA lets a person run a prostitution ring, sometimes they let them smuggle drugs, sometimes they let them launder money because they need bankers to launder money. These are all individuals the CIA can deny work for them.

"Bradley was a drug dealer. Period. Paragraph. End of Report," Daddy's best friend and lawyer Dick Crane said adamantly. I question Dick's strong reaction because he said he never met my uncle. Daddy's attorney, with no seeming connection to the players, certainly appeared to have a dog in this fight. I believe his dog was the FBI, that glorious institution that gave him an illustrious career.

"He got caught and they used him," Dick continued, "and then finally when the DEA, I'm guessing the DEA, and maybe the Bureau. But the Bureau doesn't have drug jurisdiction, the DEA does. They're the only ones, they're the sole ones that have drug jurisdiction. It used to be the BNDD (Bureau of Narcotics and Dangerous Drugs) but it's the same thing, it's a rose by any other name. They have drug jurisdiction, and they have exclusive drug jurisdiction. They work with all agencies to gather intelligence but they're the ones who bring down the drug dealers. With the aid of other government agencies such as the FBI, maybe the CIA, maybe the Defense Department. The Defense Department has its own intelligence agency apart from the CIA, they do the same thing but they're under different roofs. So, Bradley was a drug dealer who got caught and they used him, and they squeezed him. And the reason he went to jail and the reason you can tell he wasn't a major CIA player, intelligence player, is they did nothing. They let him sit in jail. They moved him around. I know he said that they moved him."

How naïve of someone as intelligent and experienced as Dick Crane to think the CIA does not routinely disavow people. I asked him about Gary Webb, the author of *Dark Alliance*, the investigative reporter that broke the story about the CIA bringing cocaine into California. Webb was a trailblazing journalist who unearthed the fact that the CIA was blanketing the gang-infested neighborhoods with drugs, creating the crack epidemic in order to fund the fight against the Nicaraguan Sandinista communist government.

"I don't believe that," Dick said. "I know there's stuff out there being said like that. I don't believe it for a second. The people on the ground in the intelligence agencies are some of our finest. They're not rogue. I mean there's an occasional rogue agent of course, but for the most part they're really stand-up people."

"That's a crock of shit," Doug Valentine countered when I told him what Dick said. "They may go to church, they may be pro-abortion rights, but they'll slit the throat of an eight-year-old kid. The CIA creates secret armies out of boys who are fourteen, fifteen and sixteen years old in foreign countries so that they can take over gold mines and diamond mines and opium fields. They assassinate people overseas. They extort them. They blackmail them to do their dirty work and it hurts their families. It just doesn't hurt them. They use and discard generals in America and congress people. It pervades the society in a way that has a general affect and has had a general affect over the last seventy-five years of what the media thinks it can say and what it doesn't want to say. It prohibits everybody from speaking openly about things."

I asked Dick why he thought Brad would have been moved from prison to prison, over one hundred and thirty times. "That was probably because the DEA wanted to keep him out of the hands of the CIA," Dick replied, proving my entire point. Chances are he recognized that as well because he doubled down, talking faster and more furious, spinning my head in circles, reminding me why he is a wildly successful attorney. "The DEA prosecuted him for drugs. He went to jail on drug charges because he was a drug dealer. Period. Paragraph. And when they put him jail, probably the intelligence agencies, whichever one he was working with or maybe he was working with more than one. The intelligence agencies would try to spring him so they moved him around so they couldn't do it. The Bureau of Prisons cooperated. Bureau of Prisons is part of The Department of Justice, so is the FBI, so is the DEA now... used to be part of the treasury."

The CIA did not want the DEA, FBI or any other agency to know what they were doing. They can't have on record the many illegal ways they gather intelligence or how money is raised for various operations. My uncle did their bidding. When he was caught, he was already programmed to think it was part of the deal he made with that devil. Soldiers make a decision to put their lives in the hands of the government in pursuit of a cause. How they ultimately feel about their sacrifice is an individual matter. Brad blames only himself and takes full responsibility.

Most government agents who advance swiftly up the ranks never set foot in a foxhole. I wonder how they feel about their soldiers' sacrifices. Those who sit in air-conditioned rooms and direct a 'handler' to communicate with an 'operative' to put him or herself in a life-threatening situation seem to conveniently turn off their conscience. They know full well if that man or woman is caught, they will disavow any knowledge of the operation. I suppose they would tell us they are saving lives and no doubt they are, but the United States military creates their own brand of fanatics, their own brand of suicide bomber. Perhaps it happens so subtly over time the party being brainwashed is hardly aware of what has transpired.

What pops into my mind is walking with Mamma and Uncle Brad out of a small movie theatre downtown in Southern Pines around 2008. We had just seen *The Good Shepherd* with Matt Damon, a drama about a young CIA operative. Uncle Brad came out white as a sheet and completely silent. Mamma asked her brother what was wrong. "That is what they do," Uncle Brad told her. "They completely take away your life."

My uncle began that life of secrets when he chose to join the elite force, glamorized in his mind from the time he was a young teenager at the Sewanee Military Academy in the 1960s. He chose to protect and serve in a much shadier way than the soldier in fatigues we see out in the open. He took up a life of lies when he chose to work for the CIA with the mindboggling caveat that no one would know what was going on, even the other guys on the playing field. It was a daring sport where participants die on a regular basis.

"It does make sense to me about Brad helping a government agency attack the drug kingpins," Uncle Earl, Brad's younger brother and former business partner acknowledged. "I never saw Brad ever use drugs. I don't see anyone being brought up in our house would have ever considered using drugs. Alcohol yes, drugs no. I was always curious why Brad did not have a U.S.–based or foreign military assignment after his basic training in the Marines. It was like he may have been recruited right out of Marine basic training."

Douglas Valentine, scholar of these private sectors, knew of Brad Bryant and maintains a less forgiving attitude. "The whole idea of anybody who had been a Marine and was dealing with organized crime," Doug told me, "thinking that the CIA was going to somehow protect him and not use him is very naïve at best."

It is Doug's opinion is that some people blind themselves to the deeply criminal and degenerate things happening within the CIA. Valentine talks of Army colonels and generals who told him the CIA offered them a nice contract, but they had too much knowledge to accept such an offer. These men had seen them "screw other generals and colonels," so they refused.

"I'm not being judgmental," Doug said kindly during our chat on the subject. "Let me just give you one more thought about it, to try to help you understand what I'm saying. I'm reading a book called *Hild*, (by Nicola Griffith) which was written about a seventh century girl who lived in East Angles in England. She later became a saint but she's a pagan in the beginning of it and she's a seer for the king, for King Edwin. She has an Irish priest who's a friend of hers and she wants him to deliver letters to her sister and he said, 'I just got back from a trip. I want to wait two weeks.' She says, 'I'm the king's seer, the king gives me whatever I want. If you don't deliver these letters, I'm going to have you whipped and there's nobody who can stop me.' And the guy says to her, 'I say to you truly, you have to learn how to stop yourself.' You know there's something about Brad where he couldn't stop himself. And that's a fatal flaw. He went to prison, and he did his time and now he can tell the story but to sugar coat it does not help. He's responsible for what he did. He got involved with people and forces that were beyond his control and why do you do that? I don't want things to get out of my control. If I meet somebody on the street and they say I'll give you a hundred dollars to take this bag to that guy standing on the corner, I say no. Brad felt there was something for him or enough for him to dispel his better judgment and go work for these people when they asked him to carry the bag across the street. He did it. He gave up control of his own fate and his ability to decide whether he was being deceived or not for some reason. He should have known better. You can't do this stuff. He'd been a Marine and Marines know that there's some risk involved in stepping outside the boundaries of what's permissible. He did it consciously. So, in a way he's both a victim and he's self-sabotaging. The fact that things about him are admirable, well sure it's true. You can be a good guy, a good person and still sabotage yourself. Like the girl sitting in that picture you sent me," Doug referred to a picture of my father with Lee Chagra in a booth in Circus Maximus Showroom at Caesar's Palace circa 1975. Lee holds a scantily clad redhead on his knee. "The young girl sitting on Lee Chagra's lap," Doug said. "Do they know better? Do they know it's a short time gig? People do things they shouldn't do."

CHAPTER
TWENTY-THREE

Cousins

Larry Bryant, Mamma and Uncle Brad's first cousin, is a multi-decorated veteran with five tours in Vietnam under his belt. Larry put on a uniform when he was ten years old and didn't take it off until he was forty and retired in 1979. "It was a military life," Larry says. "It was God, Flag and Country."

At age thirty-eight, Larry was stationed at the Nellis Air Force Base and in charge of half a million acres in the state of Nevada. Fifty miles north of Las Vegas is Indian Springs, the atomic test site. Once you go through the atomic test site you reach Groom Lake, which they call Area 51. The government owned the land so they could control all clandestine operations. Larry talked to me about simulating Russian air defense and his involvement in the secret development of the U-2 spy plane and the SR-71. The equipment he worked on was stolen from the Russians during the Cold War. There were radars, tanks, trucks, missiles, and a dozen Russian airplanes. His job was to teach the good guys how to beat the bad guys.

"It was a chess match to see how we could beat 'em," Larry explains. "You know when you have somebody five times bigger than you, you have to be smarter and that's what we tried to do was be smarter."

Larry has had a rough life. His father, my grandfather Gene Bryant's younger brother, Earl, died at thirty of alcoholism. He remembers his father's funeral at Milward Funeral Home in Lexington when he was five years old. Larry's mother Christine got out of the car and left him there. When he asked her why she would leave him in the car, she told him if he had any memories of his father, she didn't want that to be one. That was the only thing he ever thanked her for. "My mom was a mean alcoholic," Larry said plainly. "I had alcoholics on both sides and I just worry myself sick what's going to happen to my bunch. She was a fifth of vodka a day drunk and a mean one."

Widowed Christine dumped young Larry in Midway with her parents, Ada and Louis Yount. She got her own place in Lexington, coming and going as she pleased while her son attended Midway School. Louis Yount was Midway, Kentucky's fire chief, and became Larry's father for all intents and purposes. He refers to his grandparents as saints. Larry believes the event that sent him to Military school was when

Louis got him a BB gun. Christine came to visit, drunk, and raised holy hell when she saw her son with the gun. Larry's grandfather ignored her, saying the child was under his supervision.

"My mother would rather be dead than look bad," Larry said. "Never wrong and never sorry. She went down to Daddy Fred's." Christine pled her case to her late husband's father, my great-grandfather, Fred Bryant. Daddy Fred was still grieving the loss of his son Earl and wanted his grandson to have the best of life in whatever way he could arrange. He settled on a military academy.

"I was sitting on the side of a little bed in that military school in Millersburg," Larry recalled. "Big tears running down my face, pitch-black dark and the room was about the size of a bathroom, and I thought what did I do wrong? Of course, they gave me a tremendous education."

Larry never veered from a military life. He arrived in Nevada in 1973, two years after completing his final tour in Vietnam. It was the same year my brother Chan and I began going out to Las Vegas every summer to live with our father. I remember visiting Larry and his kids, our second cousins, in a small house deep in the Mojave Desert. There were chain-link fences, enormous equipment and military housing popping up precariously surrounded by vast emptiness. My recollection revolves around shades of brown, the faded half delirium you get when it's boiling hot outside, and long, sticky drives with nothing to see but sand from every window.

It's no wonder Larry and Daddy hooked up right away. We were family after all, a very close family even after a divorce. "When I was in Nevada, you and Chan were out there," Larry laughed. "Y'all came out to the base and Chan had everyone in card games. 'Course I knew Dan from marrying your mom. Him and your mom got married when I was still in high school. I've got pictures of the wedding. I think they got married in '59 or '60, somewhere along in there. And then course Happy was the governor and he lived in Versailles, and I lived in Midway, so I knew about him."

It becomes a matter of he said/he said when we talk about the events that sent both Brad and Larry to prison. More accurately, it is a matter of Larry said because Uncle Brad has been categorically silent but to say his cousin is a "genius, off the charts smart and brilliant at what he does." The two worked separately for the United States government, but both in covert fashions. With different skill sets, they were consequently used in entirely different ways, sent on wholly different missions. In the end, all I know for sure is at one point their missions intersected. Brad and Larry were in some way, shape or form doing something illegal via their respective government jobs, prompting both men's arrests.

Larry loses all good humor when telling his side. "I was down at Caesar's with your dad and Brad. They had something going with that Spanish guy," Larry explains in his heavy Kentucky accent, referring to the Lebanese Jimmy Chagra. "They hit at my ego, your dad and Brad. 'Do you know how to sneak an airplane through the American air defense?' Well, you know, fuck, that's what I do for a living! So, I fixed the airplane up, told the people what to do, and they did it." According to Larry, it was around 1977 when he went to New Mexico to modify the plane, meet the crew, and tell them how to work the equipment. He said they bought a plane from a man named Dempsey. In Larry's version of events, my father brought a suitcase of cash to pay for the plane.

"I think Brad said something to me like 'how do you penetrate an air defense?'" Larry repeated, "and I think I said, 'well shit, do this, do this, do this.' I think unknowingly, I gave 'em the way to smuggle in a whole airplane full of pot!"

"Was if for the Chagras?" I asked.

"I don't know who in the hell it was," Larry said. "All I remember is it was your dad and Brad, but I didn't know anybody else. Then after that, I went on about my business. You know hell, I didn't know anything about it until they come, drag me out of the house one night under arrest." Larry let out a dark chuckle, indeed several dark chuckles... long silences in between. "Oh, good Lord, I hate to admit this, I'm ashamed of myself. My only weakness was I was proud of what I was doing, and I got taken advantage of, 'do you know how to sneak through an air defense?' Well shit, I do it every day and I did, and it worked. They brought, goddamn, like I said, thousands of pounds, twelve thousand pounds. That's twenty-five million dollars' worth. I never got any benefit out of it! Nobody ever gave me any damn money! All I did was go to jail and my life got ruined."

I referenced Phillip Taubman's article in the *New York Times* about he and Brad, Libya and a weapons swap. "I'll tell you what the Libya thing was," Larry said. "I had all this Russian equipment up in the little area in Nevada. My buddy Bob Ellis had the airplane, so we had a whole Russian air defense there. The thing about Libya was they had a Russian radar there called a 'Tall King', it's just a slang word we used for the Russians, you know they had all these nicknames for all this Russian equipment. What we did is we went over to Libya and said, 'hey man, this radar is not really all that good, we'll give you a good radar and just take your old one.' We were going to do it so we could get the real thing over here. What happened was, there's an air base down in Warner Robins, Georgia and whoever was going to do the trade asked for spare parts for the thing and the red flags went up and said, hey we're not supposed to give Libya anything. This is a no-no."

The United States needs capable men like Larry Bryant. They became aware of his abilities early on and used him until he was all used up. While in the Air Force, they sent him to Vietnam five times until 1971. Larry directed B–52 strikes from the ground. Before the military had the high-tech abilities of warfare today, they needed minds like Larry to develop radar equipment that could synch up to a computer and attack from a safe distance.

Larry explains it this way, "if you're flying over a jungle, your scope just looks like jungle. There's no way you can put a bomb on a thatched hut with a radar, you just can't do it. So, what we did was we knew where the thatched hut was on a map, so we'd take the coordinates of the thatched hut on a map and put it into the computer of the radar. Then the computer and the radar knew exactly where the thatched hut was. We'd turn around and plug the radar on the airplane and direct it down to where the hut was. You'd say come left two degrees, come right, stand by, five, four, three, two, one, hack and the guy hits the button... bombs go out. So, we'd actually direct 'em to the target with these ground-based radars."

I didn't ask my mother's cousin how he felt about killing from a distance, sending bomb after bomb, day after day, month after month, year after year. Before I could form an opinion or grapple with the immensity of destruction he wreaked, he offered up his defense, "My only feeling about it was we had a 215-man outfit and they killed 22 of us. So, we didn't drop enough bombs, I guess."

I can only imagine what that does to a human psyche, a person's spirit, to see such destruction, to cause such destruction. Only those indoctrinated to be such a warrior could begin to understand. As far as I can tell, Larry has done very well moving forward after such an experience. He came back from Vietnam in 1971 and was sent to Las Vegas in 1973. Larry stayed at that post until he was sent to Leavenworth in 1979.

Many a theory was offered up in newspaper articles about Larry's life and why he ended up in a military prison in Kansas. The truth is much more practical than devious. Collecting and trading equipment from the Cold War had been Larry's job for years. At one point, he received night vision scopes from a man he knew at China Lake Air Force Base. His cousin Brad saw the night scopes and wanted them. Larry gave them to him. Turns out, they had been stolen by the man who gave them to Larry's contact at China Lake. Later that equipment was discovered in a warehouse belonging to Brad Bryant. This put Larry Bryant smack dab in the middle of Brad's clandestine world of drug smuggling for Jimmy Chagra.

The man who stole the night scopes turned government witness. They both testified against Larry and he was the only one of the three who went to jail. They were not letting go of Larry until they found out everything he knew about his cousin Brad and Jimmy Chagra. They held him in Leavenworth for six months… until they discovered he had no information.

"Six months," Larry shook his head. "But they destroyed my defense business. Nobody could hire me anymore because

I had no clearance. Then the CIA said, well we can give you a job. Do you want to go overseas and steal this shit and I said oh well, why not," he laughed as if he wanted to cry. "Me and a guy named Bob Ellis. Bob Ellis was the chief of maintenance of the airplanes, and I was chief of maintenance of the radars, we had known each other in the military, and we formed a company to get this military equipment for 'em. 'Course you know, that's the government for you, I had a passport and job and everything."

"So, after you went to jail," I attempted to clarify, "that's when you went to work for the CIA?"

"Yeah!" he laughed. "One of the guys that worked up there, his name was Woody Elliston, he was a CIA operative. What I did after I retired from the Air Force was I would go to all these foreign countries and get parts and pieces of equipment for the stuff that we had... a jet engine for the jet airplane, a tube for the Russian radar, a motor for something. In other words, my job was to go and get these spare parts to keep the stuff running that we already had. There was a place in London, a company called Zaerix, and they specialized in Russian vacuum tubes. You know years ago, before transistors, they had vacuum tubes. The radios and everything had vacuum tubes in it and this company had Russian vacuum tubes. God I would go over there and buy the place out," he laughed. "Shippin' 'em all back to the states. I went to Poland, and I went to... oh God everything... Romania, Czechoslovakia, all those Russian places and get pieces and parts for the stuff we needed in the states."

This was all funded by the government, by the CIA. Larry did not have to disguise himself. He wore slacks and a t-shirt for these operations. "I've got all the letters here saying that

I was a nice guy and all this stuff," Larry said. They gave him a hero medal. He wrote a paper that said that he could trace all of the Russian radar development down to two people and then he named those two people. "The CIA I think was going to trigger 'em to be shot or something," Larry said. "I felt bad about it afterwards."

Larry wrote a memoir, *Diary of a Cold War Veteran* to honor his friend Bob Ellis. Bob's wife had killed him in Las Vegas. She spent only thirty-six months in jail for the murder. Larry said she promised the prosecutor she wouldn't mention what Larry and Bob were doing. "They cut her a deal," Larry laughs ominously. "You know if you can pull strings to work with the CIA, then you can shoot somebody and kill 'em and nobody says shit." Larry's nose was stopped up by this time. He loves his friend Bob with all his heart, with all the passion you see between men who were literally in the trenches together.

Larry is uncomfortable with me writing about the events that caused such division and heartache for so many of our family members. Even so, he arrived at my doorstep with a box of his grandfather, Fred Bryant's treasured photographs and documents. Larry thought I would be the best keeper of my great grandfather's most precious memories and our family's legacy. It didn't remove the sting of my investigation. "It's an old country adage and you'll understand it," Larry said. "My Grandfather Yount in Midway said you can walk out into a field, a cow field, and you can see a pile of cowshit laying there on the ground and it's been there for a while, it's crusted over, and it doesn't smell… but you take a stick and you stir it up and it'll start to stink again. That's my feeling. I don't want to go through it again."

It surprised me to learn that Larry never crossed paths with Jimmy or Lee Chagra. His social interactions with Dan Chandler in Las Vegas were limited to favors my father happily bestowed upon all Kentucky friends and relatives who made their way out west. "Your dad would give me tickets to shows," Larry said. "I went to see Cher. I'd go down there, and he'd give me a ticket or something. I just thought it was the greatest thing in the world." When I asked if he ever met the men that were, in a not so roundabout way, his downfall, Larry replied, "I never met a Chagra," as if referring to some rare species, "wouldn't know one if I saw one."

I tell Larry about our deep entanglements with the Chagra family, about my warm impressions of Lee and Chan's friendship with Leader. I tell him that the small condo we lived in behind the Hilton, the one where Chan and I spent every summer and holiday, served as a hiding place.

"Oh, my Lord in heaven," Larry shook his head. "That was dangerous, I mean hell you could have been used as hostages. Those people are ruthless. They're drug dealers!"

CHAPTER
TWENTY-FOUR

Drew's Dirty World

Drew Thornton was conspicuously absent during Bradley Bryant's arrest. He wasn't necessarily a person of interest surrounding the fall of the Chagra empire. He wasn't among the slew of agents conducting their not-so-government-sanctioned activities at the China Lake Naval Base. The pair had been stalwart partners in covert maneuvers and all things otherwise secretive. The two loved and trusted each other like brothers. I can only imagine it was a time of anger, betrayal, and intense paranoia when their friendship took a bad turn.

I was surprised not to find a trace of those emotions when I talked to my uncle about his longtime friend. From where Brad sits, looking back on his life in his late seventies, he carries only fond memories of Drew. He doesn't remember the precise occasion things went awry but does acknowledge there came a time when Thornton was not the partner he once was. I pressed for an answer. What straw broke the camel's back? What made him decide to cut ties?

"What made me decide to cut ties?" Uncle Brad repeated my question, caught off guard. "Drew was more of a… I thought more careless. For example, I was not at all involved with drugs themselves. Drew was more casual about that, I guess you could say. And I was not. We didn't agree about everything all the time. He became more infatuated with the money involved and I was not. Obviously, we had to make sufficient funds that had to demonstrate what we were doing properly, and you couldn't do what we were doing unless you had sufficient funds to do it."

I continued to strive for clarity, to make sense in my own mind, verification that both men considered the drug smuggling a CIA mission. I knew this whole exercise had originated in that motel off I-65 when Brad and Drew were twenty-five years old, before smuggling drugs for Chagra became an integral part of getting information the CIA wanted.

"Oh yeah, that was the foundation of everything," my uncle patiently restated once again. Then in seeming disbelief at how confounding this mission became, he continued, "you kind of become so absorbed in it. It just… I mean there are so many… it's going in so many directions simultaneously to accomplish the goal and you don't really know what the goal is. You know you have to get to this individual, to get to this individual, to get to this individual and gaining confidence. Drew and I disagreed about the Chagras. After that it became complicated."

"Did Drew part ways with the CIA and just go rogue?" I asked.

"Pretty much," Uncle Brad said resignedly. "At the end. He had to step out, and uh, I don't uh… I never accepted that person. I just never thought he was not there with me if things got tough."

"Did you ever think Drew was dangerous?"

"No," he said. "Hell no."

Many people believe Andrew Carter Thornton did become dangerous. While Brad had his separate life and business in Philadelphia with my uncles Earl and Joel, Drew was enjoying his power as a lawyer and police officer in Lexington. He joined the force in 1968 and then the city's first ever drug task force in 1970. Thus began his own separate entanglement with a nefarious man named Bill Canan.

William Taulbee Canan of Mount Sterling, Kentucky loathed the anti-war movement as much as Drew. Both men had received Purple Hearts for their military service, Thornton for the U.S. intervention of the Dominican Republic and Canan for Vietnam. They were vehemently opposed to the peace and love, hippy philosophy of their day. "I joined the police department to change it," Bill Canan said of his plan to alter the culture from the inside out. "I wanted to bring in positive forces, rather than negative." He skyrocketed to the upper echelon of law enforcement as President of Lexington's Fraternal Order of Police.

Drew's new friend, Canan fell as quickly as he rose. The long-haired undercover officer's reputation became tarnished when he was accused of dastardly police brutality. He was alleged to have participated in breaking and entering, ransacking citizen's homes, beating people up and incarcerating them with trumped up charges. He was suspended from duty after lunging at the chief of police, causing a raucous in the station. The Lexington narcotics squad was clearly doing more than confiscating drugs.

"They were gun running," said Alex Sanders, filmmaker, and grandson of Kentucky State Capital Archivist Alex Sanders Jr. "They were selling guns, that's what they did back in the eighties. They would fly down to South America and trade guns for marijuana. Then they picked up and started selling cocaine. They were flying out of Kentucky at the Bluegrass Airport. Back then there was no security, there were hardly any people that watched, they were smuggling cocaine. They were getting the guns… taking guns from the police department."

In April 1979, a Fayette County Grand Jury began a probe into the corruption of the police department, namely Drew Thornton, Bill Canan and a third running buddy, Henry Vance. A serial column in the *Lexington Herald Leader* in 1989, "Birds of a Feather" by Valerie Honeycutt uncovered an indisputable time devoid of rules for the men in blue. Special FBI agent Jim Huggins described Thornton, Canan and Vance as a "rogue group that pretty much skirted the law and did a lot of questionable things in enforcing drug laws around the University of Kentucky campus and the Lexington community. They were allegedly involved in planting drugs on suspects, stealing drugs out of evidence lockers and reselling them."

Another character woven into Drew's dirty world was Mike Kelly. Wallace McClure "Mike" Kelly was a large-scale drug dealer who owned a gun store in Richmond, Kentucky. Like Brad and Drew, Mike attended Henry Clay High School in Lexington. Mike had a federal license to buy, ship and sell firearms, with a side gig providing customers with fake licenses, phone scramblers and other handy items. Kelly is reported to have knocked off pharmacies with Henry Vance. The two supposedly made fake LSD tablets to replace the real LSD they stole from the police department's evidence locker.

Mike Kelly was a survivalist. He stockpiled weapons, ammunition, and food, preparing for anarchy. "When you have monetary collapse," Kelly stated according to the Honeycutt article, "you're gonna have anarchy first. You're gonna have raids on all the food stores. Many, many people are going to be killed. The food stores and the sporting goods stores are going to be the first ones that's hit. That's the way people are. I'm a pretty fair chemist. I usually keep a pretty good stockpile of ammunition. I have quite a few weapons. I'm proficient with quite a few weapons, not necessarily firearms."

My mind goes to the insurrectionists who stormed the capital on January 6th, 2021. The rioters were comprised largely of survivalists like Kelly. He would have been a hero or at least a great source for the Oath Keepers, the Proud Boys and other doomsday preppers. These groups await, crave, and push for political and societal collapse to mobilize their blood, sweat and tear-bought communities. Michael Flynn, Lieutenant Army General and National Security Advisor to former President Trump recommended declaring martial law. Famously pictured with the Oath Keepers, Flynn's motto was "overthrow and overturn" as he spread dangerous QAnon conspiracy theories. White nationalist extremists are riddled with police officers and military men who, like Kelly, are proficient with quite a few weapons.

Bonnie Kelly, Mike's buxom, bleached blond wife from Tick Ridge, Kentucky was also familiar with fire power. Mike was convicted of smuggling marijuana in Florida and prosecuting attorney Eugene Berry was known to be tough on drug traffickers. On January 16th, 1982, in Port Charlotte, Florida, Bonnie waltzed up to the front door of the state prosecutor who was set to throw the book at her husband and shot him dead in his front hallway. Henry Vance provided the murder weapon.

True crime television series, *Prosecutors in Search of Justice* tells the story of Bonnie Kelly's plot to kill Eugene Berry. The episode entitled "Deadly Revenge" describes how Bonnie carried out the murder. Eugene Berry is described as a no-nonsense prosecutor who dedicated his life to incarcerating felons having anything to do with sellers, traffickers, or users of drugs. Just like the assassination of Texas Federal Judge John Wood, here was another weighty lawman with the power to put drug offenders away for life, meeting his end at the hand, or through the pockets, of drug dealers. In a painstaking investigation of the Berry killing, Florida authorities found their murderess and uncovered the scheme. It originated in Lexington, Kentucky and had everything to do with two key players in Drew's world, Mike Kelly and Henry Vance. Bonnie is currently serving a life sentence for the crime.

Bill Canan went to jail in 1993 for cocaine trafficking, carrying a fake badge and harassing a witness. They found in his possession papers on how to build bombs. "The thing about bombs is they go off after you're gone," Drew's running buddy supposedly said. "The bad thing about it is people die." Canan did fifteen years and got out of prison in 2008. In a strange twist of fate, he died the same week as Henry Vance in March of 2020.

Then there was Triad Farm, a piece of rural land on the Kentucky river partly owned by Drew. It was believed to be a training camp for terrorists, mercenaries and drug runners. They are said to have been practicing soldier of fortune training and that Triad Farm was a camp for survivalist like the ex-military man Benicio Del Toro played in *The Hunted*. Tommy Lee Jones portrayed his skilled teacher in the film, the man who made Benicio's character the assassin he was. Neighbors of Triad heard gunshots and had strange sightings of camouflage men in the area. There is much speculation and romanticism surrounding their mercenary world.

It's impossible to discern every piece of fact from fiction. I fall victim to lapping up rumors as well, assuming the Valerie Honeycutts, Dominic Dunnes and FBI's Bill Huggins of the world have proof of what they say about Bill Canan, Henry Vance, Mike and Bonnie Kelly. With a clear understanding of the insatiable hunger for gossip, suffering from the affliction myself, I must remember while researching the many crimes and characters of the era, the so-called 'experts' might not know the truth even while looking official in their offices and outfits.

"Crooked cops, cocaine and conspiracy as bluebloods go bad," Dominic Dunne reported gravely in a dark suit, hands clasped behind a desk in his beautiful East Coast home. The mythical version of Bradley Bryant, Andrew Thornton and

The Company stuck like Gorilla glue. The truth is far more complicated than Dominic Dunne could ever imagine. Like Jack Nicholson screamed in *A Few Good Men*, "You can't handle the truth!" When you sign up for the military like my grandfather, Gene Bryant and his brother Earl, like Uncle Brad and his brother Earl and their cousin Larry, like Drew and his friend Bill Canan, you sign up to be killed. If you become a Marine, you are often the first line of defense. It is my understanding that when you join the Marines Corps more than any other force, you are initially broken down so thoroughly, you have no one to depend on but another Marine. You go in a son, a daughter, a brother and come out a family member of the United States Marines. All of these men might have been very different had the military not been so involved in the creation of their character.

Bluegrass Sons

CHAPTER
TWENTY-FIVE

"The sins of the father are to be laid upon the children..."
—William Shakespeare

The creation of the Chagras' character was cut from an entirely different cloth, dating back to their parents native Lebanon. It was El Paso, 1988. "Look at the love she found in me," lilted through the speakers of the church. Leader was so handsome on his wedding day. Lee Chagra's only son was beautiful really, with his wide, brown, doe eyes. His best man was Joseph Daniel "Chan" Chandler Jr., my big brother who sauntered down the aisle with a bridesmaid, dashing in his tux. Leader smiled and winked at Chan, the secrets of their youth ever-present. They were twenty-five years old. Chan and Leader hit it off immediately from the moment Daddy delivered us to their hotel suite. The two fourteen-year-olds running down to the casino to find slot machines out of the camera's view.

"I love this town, Kentucky!" Eighteen-year-old Leader shouted, head popping out of the sunroof of my brother's BMW. He first came to Lexington to visit Chan in high school, and they passed out Caesar's gold medallions to the wide-eyed kids at Sayre. They shared a sense of humor and developed a matching tone of voice, hand gestures and swagger, moving through the world with warmth and a smooth gentleness that exuded confidence at a primal level. While Leader favored his father Lee, Chan got most of his good looks from our maternal grandfather, Gene Bryant.

Joe Chagra, Leader's uncle, read a prayer at the service. "Treat everyone with equal kindness," he recited. "Never be condescending but make real friends with the poor, never repay evil with evil but let everyone see that you are interested only in the highest ideals. Do all you can to live at peace in this world. This is the word of the Lord."

Almost a decade had passed since Lee Chagra, Leader's beloved father was murdered in cold blood sitting at his desk in his El Paso office. Lee's brother Jimmy was in jail, convicted in 1979 for heading a massive drug smuggling ring. Jimmy Chagra plead guilty in 1984 to attempted murder of a federal prosecutor. Leader's Uncle Joe, the man delivering those words from the bible, spent six and a half years in prison himself, also convicted in 1979 for conspiracy to kill Federal Judge John Wood. Joe was the chief prosecuting witness that brought down the hit man, Charles Harrelson. Joe admitted to a heavy cocaine habit and claimed his actions were in large part due to a negative influence his brothers Jimmy and Lee inflicted on him.

The wedding ceremony seemed like a new lease on life, a new beginning for the Chagra clan, the worst behind them. "It was like a scene out of *The Godfather*," my mother recalled of the nuptials. She wasn't referring to the tragedies that had befallen the Chagras, but the outpouring of familial love. As faces were grabbed and kisses planted, there was a deep sense of devotion in that room. Leader looked like a teenager, joy bubbling up from his insides. The bride, Dina Ellington, soon to be Dina Chagra, had stars in her own big brown eyes. She wore a classic 80s wedding dress, enormous snow-white poufy sleeves and a long veil beaded with pearls. Her curly dark hair matched each one of her bridesmaids.

I watch the video over and over. The heartaches that preceded are nowhere in sight, the ones to follow, unfathomable. The hopefulness shown on Chan, Leader and Dina's faces, those dreams and assumptions of a happily ever after were all in vain. My heart goes out to the friends and lovers on that joyous occasion on a hot El Paso summer afternoon.

William Shakespeare would have us believe that the sins of the father are to be laid upon the children, so would whoever penned passages in the Bible inferring the same generational doom. I don't personally subscribe to such a notion, but it seems to have held true in this instance as the wedding party went down one after another, after another. The first to go was the lovely young bride. Dina died of cancer four years later. Soon after that, Joe Chagra died in a car crash.

Within five years, my big brother lost his battle with addiction, Leader's name on the tip of his tongue. "If I could just talk to Leader," Chan said in the living room of our father's small condo behind the Hilton, moments before making a fatal mistake. He was beyond drunk on vodka and high on crack cocaine when he searched the eyes of his twenty-one-year-old girlfriend for one last bit of hope after a horrific drug and alcohol fueled day spiraling downward. He and the young girl who had flown in from Kentucky had been watching *Bugsy*, where the mobster plays Russian roulette. She didn't know what was happening when Chan rushed into the bedroom and returned with our father's gun, announcing he was going to "do a Bugsy Siegal." In quick succession, he took all the bullets out but one, spun the chamber, put the gun to the back of his head and fired. The girlfriend on her first trip to Vegas watched her handsome boyfriend fall to the ground. The traumatized girl told the police that Chan's eyes flashed with the shocking realization he had pushed fate too far.

I was with Chan just two weeks before at Daddy Gene's funeral. He looked gorgeous in his long cashmere coat, standing tall and strong above our grandfather's gravesite. Moving a few feet to his right, he hovered over Daddy Gene's brother's grave. Earl Bryant had died on May 22nd, 1945. He was thirty years old. I heard Chan say hauntingly, prophetically, "I beat you by two weeks." Indeed, my precious brother was gone two weeks later, May 22nd, 1993. The depth of our generational inheritance must be more than coincidental. Chan and his maternal great uncle both died at the exact same age on the exact same day, both due to their alcoholism. The correlation is other worldly.

At my brother's funeral, there was no one I felt closer to than Leader. I remember standing at the door of his hotel suite where everyone gathered the night before the service. Leader sat on the bed crossed legged, smiling through tears, holding court over Chan's other friends. Heartbroken, we looked at each other. No words were needed. It was unspoken, telepathic. We both knew what a treasure we had lost. Chan is as much a part of me today as he was then. I would bet my life he still occupies a hefty section of Leader's heart and mind as well.

In 1995, Leader went to prison. At that point he had lost his father, his wife, and his best friend. To add to the catastrophic nature of his life thus far, Leader was betrayed by his aunt. His mother's sister arranged the setup, urging her nephew to make one small drug exchange in his kitchen. The sting was a feather in the cap of Texas authorities. They were ready to throw ten books at the Chagra family for everything Leader's father and uncles had done. For the sins of the father, they punished the son to the full extent of the law. Leader served ten years in maximum security prison.

My mind goes to the custom-made bracelets we all had, gifts from the Chagras. Some were made of elephant hair; others had the word *"FREEDOM"* written in 18k gold italics. I think of the St. Christopher medal Leader's mom JoAnnie gave Chan to keep him safe. He kept that medal in his wallet his entire life. Chan adored JoAnnie and held her on a pedestal, a mother figure personifying loyalty to blood and family. It was a kinship my big brother craved. With our immediate household broken, Chan romanticized this Lebanese tribe who laughed and ate and celebrated life in their El Paso compound just yards from the Mexican border.

I went to visit Leader in prison in 2009. It was a colorless, one-story dormitory building with a small, private visitors' patio. Beyond the short concrete wall in which we were enclosed there was nothing but reddish yellow sand as far as the eye could see. It didn't feel like there was heavy security keeping these men captive in the middle of this Texas desert, but I suppose there was. Leader came out beaming, wearing the same type of khaki button-down shirt and pants Uncle Brad had worn in prison so many years before. Confident and cocky as ever, Leader could have been Hugh Hefner in a silk robe with that swagger and spirit, that irrepressible spirit. He leaned over and hugged me. It was like my brother hugging me. So similar was the manner in which they held themselves, letting out that high giggly laugh that was easily accessible no matter the circumstance. I often wonder who came up with the mannerisms first, the tonality of speech and the way they moved their bodies. Eventually they morphed into the same kind of person, brothers from another mother, an American kid from Kentucky and a Lebanese kid from El Paso.

CHAPTER
TWENTY-SIX

Drew's Final Flight

Joseph Daniel Chandler Jr. and Lee Chagra Jr.'s teenage bond lasted a lifetime, just as Bradley Bryant and Andrew Thornton's did. While adolescent, Brad and Drew received an education at Sewanee Military Academy in order and discipline. Chan and Leader got their education at Caesar's Palace, learning literally the opposite. For teenage Brad and Drew it was boots on the ground, exercise, and training, teenage Chan and Leader got Blackjack tables, room service and showgirls. Brad and Drew learned military drills in record time, Chan and Leader learned to gamble, place bets on the sports book and pilfer drugs from their fathers' stashes. Both bonds were never to be broken, both partnerships lasted until one was dead and the other in prison.

Five years after Bradley Fred Bryant went to prison, Andrew Carter Thornton II jumped from a small twin-engine Cessna to his death, landing on a driveway in Knoxville, Tennessee. It was September 11th, 1985. Hours later, law enforcement investigators attempted to decipher why a man in very expensive jump clothing would be skydiving in the middle of the night. On his body, authorities discovered several thousand dollars in cash and two Kentucky driver's licenses with Drew's picture, one for Andrew Thornton, another for Andrew Bourbon. A large black bag was attached to his body holding thirty-four small parcels marked USA, each containing a kilo of unprocessed cocaine, over eighty pounds, the street value of almost twenty million dollars. In his pocket there was a note with the epigram, a quote attributed to General George Patton: "There is only one tactical principal not subject to change: It is to inflict the maximum amount of wounds, death and destruction on the enemy in the minimum amount of time."

In addition to his warrior's words to live by, drugs and money, Drew jumped out of the plane with a backpack full of weapons. There were various handguns, a fully loaded semi-automatic 9mm as well as a Derringer. Officers at the time noted a Derringer was typically used by someone involved in a deep cover operation. Many cops apparently preferred this as their backup weapon. Drew also had a pair of military grade, non-traceable night vision goggles and a notebook with numeric codes no one was able to decipher.

They found gold Krugerrands, South African coins, and Teflon-coded bullets, 'cop-killers', named for their ability to pierce through bullet proof vests and other body armor.

Surprisingly, Drew had only minor injuries apparent on his face and body. There was a cut to his chin and mouth, his nose had been bleeding. He was clutching the rip cord. The main parachute never deployed. The emergency shoot opened on its own, but not soon enough to break his fall. Investigators surmised that as he jumped from the plane, he must have struck the wing and was knocked temporarily unconscious. This caused the blow to his chin. Other injuries are thought to have come from the duffel bags battering him on the way down. They believed that once he regained consciousness, he was unaware of how close to the ground he was and pulling his emergency shoot flipped him on his back. The medical examiner ruled it an accident.

A Georgia forest ranger later found two black duffel bags caught in the trees, obviously dropped from a plane. They were identical to the ones strapped to Drew's body. The bags contained 150 more kilos of cocaine. Still, more bags were found in the Chattahoochee National Forest and in Cherokee County, Georgia. The plane was found crashed in the North Carolina Mountains.

"He was a 007 paramilitary type personality," said one narcotics detective of Drew Thornton. "An adventurer driven by adrenaline rushes." It was a lifetime of risk taking from his countless jumps as an Army paratrooper, who knows how many years as a renegade CIA operative, time as a rogue police officer, and many daring trips to and from South America trafficking drugs. It seems most extraordinary that what finally took him out was a simple miscalculation.

The last man to see Andrew Thornton alive was the other passenger on that Cessna. Bill Leonard is a man Drew met at a Lexington Karate studio. They had sparred and had breakfast several times before the man agreed to work as Drew's bodyguard. "Hey Bill, I'm going over to the Bahamas to meet a couple of guys to talk about some things and I need somebody to watch my back," Drew said, according to Leonard's recount of events in the *Knoxville News Sentinel*. "I'll pay you for it."

Leonard tells a story of a harrowing flight instead to Colombia. They landed in a swamp and were cajoled by machine-gun-toting *federales*. They ate parrot and Bill got food poisoning. He threw up on the raucous flight back to the States. They discovered they were being chased and Drew instructed Bill to throw the cocaine bags out of the window and then informed him he would have to jump himself. The karate cohort jumped successfully and survived. Drew followed and did not.

Bluegrass Sons

Chan Chandler and Leader Chagra, Derby, Louisville, Kentucky

CHAPTER
TWENTY-SEVEN

"Mammas don't let your babies grow up to be cowboys..."
—Ed and Patsy Bruce

I was a kid in the 1970s, then a teenager. What a heady experience it must have been for Daddy and his girlfriend to have been in their thirties and early forties, feet planted firmly in the wild west, minds formed in the fifties. Las Vegas was completely alien to her Philadelphia and his Kentucky. Dan Chandler and Delores were young, strong, and able to choose. If your proclivity was to be adventurous, which theirs happened to have been, the 1970s in America, specifically out west, was an altogether unique time and place to sow one's wild oats.

Youth is a mystery until we are on the back side of it. If we are lucky enough to survive long enough to reflect on the period, we assumed control over our destiny, we ease up on the reins. Maybe we let go at forty, maybe fifty or maybe, like my brother, we go screaming out of the world the way we came in. Maybe we are forced to let go because of illness or accident. Maybe we are thrown into prison, locked up and forced to stop, take a look at what our life really is, what our actions and motivations really caused.

Sometimes I wake up heartbroken all over again. I turn a corner, fold a sheet and it hits me, a wave of heartache so deep I relive the darkest aspects of my brother's life. I remember equally and just as clearly the countless adventures, joy, elation and pure love he experienced in his thirty years. I don't think Daddy is to blame for his difficulty in grasping and hanging on to a more stable existence. I don't think Uncle Brad is to blame. I do, however, think the world my father and uncle embraced is to blame, that world of gamblers, gangsters and drugs. No telling what went on in Chan's developing little boy brain as his role models lived out a real-life game of cowboys and Indians in front of his eyes.

Gene Ganucheau witnessed the boy becoming a man and recalls a time in Joe Namath's suite at Caesar's Palace. The famous quarterback and Dan Chandler were close friends for over forty years, and he seemed to be a mainstay in my father's world whether it be Vegas, Aspen or LA. Gene remembers an afternoon watching a ball game with Joe, Daddy and Chan in the football star's Caesar's Palace suite. He was around forty at the time and playing with the Los Angeles Rams. "We're all smoking pot," Gene recalled. "Chan was still a kid and when we left, he goes, 'Look at that. My hero, smoking pot.' It wasn't long after that Chan was smoking it too."

Gene's thoughts turned toward my mother at that point of our conversation. "Your mother is awesome, I love her," he said. "I knew her enough to know she was your all's savior from Dan. I'm not saying… Dan was the greatest guy I've ever known, you know? He would make it fun. He would find fun. That included smoking pot and doing a little cocaine. I didn't do it all the time because I had a job. I did a lot of that stuff and you probably have too. You were talking about he would look out for you guys, but he also got Chan involved in a lot of… Chan thought he was your dad because that's how… he would do things just like your dad would do but he couldn't. He couldn't. Then he got older, and he got a little cockier and you know one thing led to another. It's a shame what happened to him. I'm sorry."

I blame the existence of Las Vegas for Chan's downfall, compounded with the decadence of the time and recklessness of the players. To have your personality formed in that kind of environment is unsettling at best. "I don't know exactly what happened that day," Gene said. "I mean, I read it. I read police reports too, but when he told me I said, god that could have been me. You know how your dad was, he always had a gun."

I can't stand having a firearm in the house now. I hug the walls when a gun is in the room. I was not aware of my father's extreme carelessness, or at least until now, I didn't identify it as such. I remember him taking Chan and me out in the desert and teaching us how to shoot when I was about twelve. I fired once and was so shocked at the power of the weapon, I never held one again. There were always guns on the bed side table, in suit pockets and on the kitchen sink. I recently found a small gun holster and remembered vividly that little wool lined, leather holster which until then always held a pistol. It brought back decades of memories of that little condo in Vegas.

Before we hung up, my father's oldest Vegas running buddy, Gene Ganucheau and I spoke finally about our mutual sobriety. "I'll be seventy years old in a week and I feel like a kid," Gene said. "I haven't had a drink in 22 years. But before that I drank with the best of them, and your dad was the best of them."

I am proud of the boys on both sides of my family, those Bluegrass sons. Not a coward in the bunch. They ran towards the fire, not away from it. Women and children first. My earliest memory of my father's heroism was on Cayman Island. Walking fully clothed on the beach we looked out into the ocean and saw two hands desperately waving out by the buoy, the head was underwater tangled in the rope. Without a second of hesitation Dan Chandler tore off his suit pants and dress shirt and ran full speed into the ocean. He emerged back on shore a few minutes later holding up a man whose legs were amputated from the knee down. The man would have drowned had it not been for my courageous father.

Daddy lived ten lifetimes in his seventy years. He spent his last two, 2003 and 2004 living in the cabin next door to his older brother, Ben in Versailles, Kentucky. It is the cabin where their Baseball Commissioner father signed papers that changed the sport forever, supporting Jackie Robinson to play in the major leagues. Back home at long last, Daddy entertained friends, flew his West Coast buddies in for the Derby and hosted his famous post Derby Fried Chicken party. As usual, his events brought in all the celebrities of the moment, among them, Kenny Stabler, Chuck Norris, Toby Kieth, Bob Baffert and Anita Madden. He enjoyed life and continued to be grateful, continued, as Gene Ganucheau said, to find fun, to make fun. Daddy held court by the pool with a Scotch in one hand and a Cigar permanently dangling from his mouth right up until the end when his heart gave out. That precious organ had quite a job keeping up with his excesses. At age seventy, on my birthday, April 27th, 2004, my incomparable father went on to the other side.

During his lifetime, Daddy's older brother, Albert Benjamin Chandler II exhibited equal parts superiority and jealousy for his little brother but made up for it with undying love. Uncle Ben's last years without him were his loneliest. "I can tell you who I miss most is my brother Dan," he told me with tears in his eyes. "If I could see one person again, it wouldn't be my mom or my dad, it would be my brother Dan."

Uncle Ben was like Uncle Earl in that he followed the rule book. I don't believe it ever occurred to either of them to stray. Those Bluegrass sons were similar only in how different they were from their brothers. It was in Earl Bryant and Ben Chandler's DNA to follow the rules as much as it was in Dan Chandler and Brad Bryant's to break them. It's worth noting that Uncle Ben could no more run a casino and host a wide swath of international millionaires and celebrities than fly to the moon. By the same token, it's unimaginable that Uncle

Earl would don a pair of snakeskin boots and a dagger, fly to Colombia to pick up four hundred pounds of marijuana and land it safely in the hands of Jimmy Chagra's goons.

Uncle Brad survived those incredible days as a spy, a good guy playing hardball with bad guys. After his release from prison, he dedicated his life, as he said he would, to his family. He started his own health and wellness business with his kids called Well 4 Life. He moved to Southern Pines, North Carolina, a few miles from my mom, making the peaceful town his sanctuary. His mostly glass house was surrounded by some of the oldest longleaf pines in the country and it held a home gym where he sustained a private practice in exercise rehabilitation. Uncle Brad is immensely beloved by everyone in our family. He is beloved by me. It's hard to reconcile the man who led such a dangerous life with the one we all know. Ultimately, I believe he is a man who desperately hopes he did the right thing. He wants to believe he was on the side of good. My uncle continues to be torn about what he once perceived as his duty, spending much of every day trying to forget that part of his life. My heart breaks for his fragmented sense of duty versus morality.

In Southern Pines, Uncle Brad took special care of his mom as she had always taken special care of him. My grandmother, Angelee Bradley Bryant Chick, spent the last six years of her life at my mother's house in a hospital bed after a stroke. Mamma and Aunt Leigh carefully nurtured her. It was a brutal ending to an extraordinary life. There was no reason for this vibrant, one-of-a-kind beauty, inside and out, to hang on to this life for a moment longer. On the day we witnessed her passing from this realm to the next, I stood by as Mamma, Uncle Earl, Uncle Brad and Aunt

Leigh gathered around their mother. "Tell her you will be okay," Aunt Leigh said to her brother, Brad. "Let her know you will be okay."

With his head down, holding his mother's hand tightly, Uncle Brad said softly, "I'll be okay, Mom. I'll be okay." The moment those words left his mouth, tears poured out of his eyes and my grandmother left this world.

Erin Chandler and her grandmother, Angelee Bradley Bryant, 'Dear'

Erin Chandler

CHAPTER
TWENTY-EIGHT

"And if the house just keeps on winning, I got a wild card up my sleeve. And if love keeps giving me lemons, I'll just mix 'em in my drink. And if the whole wide world stops singing, and all the stars go dark, I'll keep a light on in my soul, keep a bluebird in my heart..."

—Miranda Lambert

J ournalists Erin Keane and Sean Cannon approached me in September of 2020 to do an interview with my uncle, Bradley Bryant. I called him and he agreed. Together, we talked to Erin and Sean on record for two hours. During that conversation memories flooded my mind and perhaps a little late to the party, I became curious. How deeply involved was my father in my uncle's secret world? How profoundly was my brother impacted by the males in our family? Taking my personal interest public flew in the face of my family's tradition of silence on the subject. While Uncle Brad trusted me and never doubted my motives, I felt pushback from other family members which was upsetting but I pressed on.

Learning more about the atmosphere I witnessed with my own eyes set the groundwork to uncover the scene from an adult perspective. It wasn't just my uncle's story. He was just a piece of the fabric that made up our family quilt. It was also my father's story, my mother's, it was Chan's and Leader's, it was Dear's and Daddy Gene's. It was a story that included Preston and Anita Madden, the Chagras and Drew Thornton. It was a story of the undeniable connection between Las Vegas and Kentucky. It was a story of our government.

My Uncle Brad remains vehemently careful not to reveal too much, not to expose a task or mission or put a single human being at risk who may still be in that world of secrecy. When allegiance is so ingrained, you never stop protecting those who answer that same call to duty. How many families are victims of this corporate strategy moving human beings around an invisible battlefield like toy soldiers? How many wives and husbands have lost spouses to a business model that repurposed their strong, capable partners into secret agents in the most dangerous parts of the world? How many loved ones have paid for information that would have been impossible to get any other way? Off they go for bits of insight and glimpses into neighboring societies, sideways down a muddy hill, only to be chalked up as collateral damage. Everyone connected to someone sworn to secrecy, trying to thwart an attack, or carry out a covert operation will feel the sting of betrayal when their family member is ignored, disavowed, or imprisoned by the very government they sacrificed their lives for.

Many young men and women feel indestructible and headstrong about a perceived purpose. Brad went into airports and train stations, marched straight to where they kept the lockers, placed a suitcase into a locker, locked it, and never went back. Everything was underground and mysterious. Partner that adrenaline rush of secrecy with youth, physical strength and the intense military training a Marine receives and you have a force to be reckoned with. It is said that to live that kind of life and to engage in the close quarters combat CIA overlords require of their operatives, it takes thirty percent training and seventy percent balls. "Yes," Uncle Brad laughs. "I was a young stud. Oh yeah, oh yeah. Yep. Yep."

Now we watch Afghanis run alongside a United States Airforce transport plane desperately trying to get out of their homeland before they are beheaded by Taliban. We see Russian soldiers rape, torture and pillage fragile and benevolent villagers during Putin's war on Ukraine. We see the ferocious, sadistic brutality Mexican drug cartels inflict on a nation of innocent citizens in Juarez and Mexico City. I recognize that there is a need for extreme training to deal with an extreme world of evil.

It may just be the nature of this earth to house equal measure lunatics and saints. Finding out how to foil plots of destruction takes the type of uncompromising loyalty to which Bradley Bryant forfeited his life. Did this change him as a human being? Absolutely. Every person charged to root out the darkest of human behavior is going to have to use a few dark instincts of their own. To kill a monster, you have to get in bed with other monsters.

"What happens if you don't, you know what I mean?" Uncle Brad asked in his own defense. "What happens next? I mean the sacrifices are unquestionably beyond description but if you don't what happens? Well, you say I'm just a number, well that's right, but there are some things we've got to do. Someone's got to do. Somewhere along the line, someone's got to do these things or bad things can happen, worse things can happen."

My uncle entered this secret world willingly, placing it above all else. Brad Bryant dove into a den of vipers and remained true to his pledge and the missions given him. Keeping these secrets for fifteen years in the field, a decade in federal prison and thirty years after, Uncle Brad never outed the CIA or any of the criminals he associated with in that alternate universe all spies live, regardless of countless and ruthless attempts from the FBI and other agencies to break him. It has been a long journey towing the party line, making decisions out of a strict, conservative code to protect family and country, finding comfort only in discipline, order, and duty. Things Brad did were daring, violent and deadly on a global scale, among them hunting down a child pornography ring in Nicaragua and smuggling thousands of pounds of marijuana for El Paso drug lord, Jimmy Chagra. Tabloid stories and a brutal reputation in his hometown pales in comparison to the real demons he lives with every day.

I asked him if he has faith in the military now, if he has faith in the CIA. "It comes down to the individuals, honey," he tells me wisely. "I think there are some really, really great people and there are some really just average people. Things happen, people are compromised, so much corruption in our politics. You sacrifice your life, honey. Basically. You don't know that when you first sign up, course you don't have any idea what you're getting involved in but... uh... you know, you think you got a mission, you think you got a purpose in your life and then it turns out it destroys your life as far as you know it."

The ultimate answer may not be satisfactory for any true piece of mind. It may be that humans, at our core, are predatory animals. Unlike a cow or zebra who has eyes on the side of their head for wider vision of potential predators, our eyes look straight ahead, easier to plunge forward and attack our prey. Perhaps there will be no end to violence on earth because it is part of our nature. We may be fighting a losing battle. There are countless men and women at this moment in the Department of Homeland Security, The Department of Justice, the CIA, FBI, DEA and our local police departments all doing their dead level best to protect the population from predators. There may be no realistic endgame if there is no realistic end to evil doers.

Finally, I asked Uncle Brad how he feels about the state of our union. "How do I feel?" he asked. "I don't know how I feel, you look at your comparison, what are you going to compare this to Russia? Nicaragua? Guatemala? You look at the stuff, as difficult as things are here, we are nothing compared, you know what I mean? You look at the tragedies and poverty and corruption and stuff like that. As bad as things are here, we don't even compare."

"What is the most dangerous country do you think?"

"Probably China," Brad says without hesitation. "Probably China. Overall, probably China."

ACKNOWLEDGMENTS

I offer my sincere gratitude to everyone who made this book possible. First and foremost, to my mother, Lynne Bryant Chandler Brown for her mighty strength, her gracious influence, her powerful love, and the endless editing sessions. Deep respect and love to my uncle, Bradley Fred Bryant for telling his story and having the courage to set the record straight. I thank my family, Earl Bryant, Leigh Bryant Stevenson, Joel Stevenson, and Larry Bryant for allowing me to interview them about a very difficult time in their lives and for their continued love and support. I appreciate the hours spent talking with the lawyers involved in the drama, Oscar Goodman, Fred Morelli and Richard P. Crane. I thank my own lawyer, Shannon Hensley. The invaluable insight from author and CIA expert Douglas Valentine was of great importance to my understanding the world in which the players played. To my local historians who offered their take on Kentucky during the era in question, Graddy Johnson, Ann Hollingsworth, Lucy Backer, Jimmy Lambert, Governor John Y. Brown and Alex Sanders, I thank you. A big hug goes to Gene Ganucheau who gave a most enlightening testimony from his unique insider's perspective. To Juni Walsh, Connie Blankenship and Jenny Marshall for being my constants. To Erin Keane for getting me started on my own research. Appreciation goes to Evan Mascagni along with his partners, Sean Cannon, Heather Schroering and Boyd Holbrook for sharing their passion. I send a lifetime of love to my little sister, Happy, the daughter of those two passionate lovers, Dan and Delores. By way of circumstances beyond our control, Happy did not grow up with Chan, Daddy and me. She may have escaped the madness of growing up with our father but regretfully missed out on so much love. Still, Happy never left our hearts and minds. We reconnected in her teens and my twenties, both recognizing the powerful Chandler gene pool, our laughs, our insecurities, our very personalities are so similar. Tanner, my nephew, and Dan Chandler's only grandson, I hope this book enlightens you. It's nothing short of a tragedy that we did not get to see you grow up. I remember Daddy's joy holding you as a baby. I see my young father in your young face, he is more a part of you than you know, and I am most certain a powerful guardian angel, cheering you on every step of the way. Love and appreciation always to my Rabbit House Press partners, Emily Wilhoit, Brooke Lee and Kristin Minter. Thank you to William Broberg, Erica Friis, Bear Parker, Patrick Wilhoit, and most importantly, John Bosch for helping us bring this story beyond the page. To my cousins, Whitney, Matthew and Ben Chandler for always giving me a soft place to land and my Bryant cousins for being the beautiful, strong, special human beings they are. Finally, I dedicate this book to my husband, Mark Thomas who I love forevermore. Thank you for insisting I tell this story.

www.ingramcontent.com/pod-product-compliance
Lightning Source LLC
Chambersburg PA
CBHW032053020426
42335CB00011B/317